S0-BSD-339

WITHDRAWN

AT THE
CROSSROADS
OF FAITH
AND REASON

AT THE
CROSSROADS
OF FAITH
AND REASON

An Essay on

PIERRE BAYLE

by

KARL C. SANDBERG

THE UNIVERSITY OF ARIZONA PRESS / TUCSON

CARL A. RUDISILL LIBRARY
LENOIR RHYNE COLLEGE

230.0924
Sa 5 a
58 066
July 1967

ABOUT THE AUTHOR

KARL C. SANDBERG has contributed articles on the origins and literature of the Enlightenment in France to *Studies in Philology* and the *Journal of the History of Philosophy*. Professor Sandberg holds a Bachelor's and a Master's degree in French from Brigham Young University and the degree of Doctor of Philosophy from the University of Wisconsin. Formerly a teacher at Duke University, he has been on the faculty of the University of Arizona in the Department of Romance Languages since 1961.

Copyright © 1966
The Board of Regents of the Universities and
State College of Arizona. All rights reserved.
LC Number 66-18531

Contents

List of Abbreviations

THE following abbreviations of Bayle's works have been used in this study. Except as noted, these works may be found in *Oeuvres diverses de M. Bayle* (La Haye, 1737), 4 vols. For a full description of these works, see the bibliography on page 115.

APDC	*Addition aux "Pensées diverses sur les comètes"* . . . *pour servir d'instruction aux juges ecclésiastiques qui en voudraient connaître.* 1694.
CC	*La Cabale chimérique.* . . . 1691.
CCR	*Chimère de la cabale de Rotterdam.* . . . 1691.
CG	*Critique générale de l'Histoire du calvinisme de M. Maimbourg.* 1682.
CP	*Commentaire philosophique sur ces paroles de Jésus-Christ: "Contrains-les d'entrer."* . . . 1686–1687.
DHC	*Dictionnaire historique et critique.* Rotterdam, 1697.
EGS	*Entretiens sur le grand scandale causé par un livre intitulé "La Cabale chimérique. . . ."* 1691.
Ec1M	"Eclaircissement sur les manichéens," in the *Dictionnaire historique et critique,* Vol. IV. 1702.
Ec1P	"Eclaircissement sur les pyrrhoniens," in the *Dictionnaire historique et critique,* Vol. IV. 1702.
FTC	*Ce que c'est que la France toute catholique sous le règne de Louis le Grand.* 1686.
LFam	*Lettres de M. Bayle à sa famille.* 1737.
NL	*Nouvelles Lettres de M. Bayle.* La Haye, 1737.
NLC	*Nouvelles Lettres de l'auteur de la "Critique générale. . . ."*
NRL	*Nouvelles de la République des Lettres.* 1684–1687.
OD	*Oeuvres diverses de M. Bayle.* La Haye, 1737.
PDC	*Pensées diverses sur la comète.* 1682.
ProjDC	*Projet et fragments d'un dictionnaire critique,* in the *Dictionnaire historique et critique,* Vol. IV. 1692.
SCP	*Supplément du "Commentaire philosophique."* . . . 1688.
SRPJ	"Suite des Réflexions sur le prétendu jugement du public," in the *Dictionnaire historique et critique,* Vol. IV. 1702.

Introduction

ONE of the revealing details of the personality of Pierre Bayle (1647–1706) is that he never married because he felt that a wife and family obligations would interfere with his studies. An erudite, a scholar, a journalist, a dialectician, he was frugal in his habits and abundant in his thoughts. He appeared to live almost entirely by the intellect, avid of news and "matière de raisonnement." His recreation during the last half of his life as a Huguenot refugee consisted of watching an occasional puppet show and gathering at infrequent intervals with friends to discuss subjects of philosophy and theology. Except for the intensity of his intellectual life, he resembled in many ways a host of other obscure erudites of the late seventeenth century.

He differed from them essentially in that he had, to use his own phrase, "assisté de près aux grands combats de la foi et de la raison." His writings on the issues of faith and reason became one of the major catalysts of the thought of the Enlightenment, and what makes them fascinating and significant today is that they are perhaps the best mirror of the intellectual battles of the late seventeenth century, when the Age of Belief was passing into the Age of Reason. In fact, it seems unlikely that the twentieth-century confrontation of the questions of belief and existence can be seen in any true perspective without taking into account this transitional period in which so many of the assumptions of modern thought took form.

The main events of Bayle's life are easily outlined. He was born the son of a Huguenot pastor in 1647 in the remote town of Carla in southwestern France. He spent his childhood and adolescence in this provincial and Calvinist environment. He was converted to Catholicism in 1669, reconverted to the Reformed Church eighteen months later, and then spent two years at the Protestant Seminary at Geneva studying for the ministry. He decided against becoming a pastor, however, spent two years as a tutor in Rouen, and then became professor of history and philosophy at the Protestant Academy at Sedan from 1676 until it was closed by Louis XIV in 1681. Joining the stream of Huguenot exiles, he went to Rotterdam where he taught in a municipal academy, began a monthly periodical of literary reviews *(Les Nouvelles de la République des Lettres),* and wrote voluminously on philosophic and religious subjects. During this period (1682–87) he was principally a Protestant polemicist, and the bulk of his writings was devoted to defending the Protestant cause against Catholic attacks. During the last sixteen years of his life he was engaged in polemics with various of his fellow Protestants, and in 1697 produced what was to become the arsenal of the *philosophe* party, the *Dictionnaire historique et critique.* He died in 1706.

But to assess the significance of these events and the intent of his writings has been much more difficult. An atheist, a deist, a skeptic, a Socinian, a liberal Calvinist, a conservative Calvinist, a libertine — all of these positions have been assigned to him(See Chapter 2), and the image of his generation has been obscured to that extent.

There has even been considerable doubt as to his correct category in chronology. He lived all of his life as a subject of Louis XIV, but in most literary manuals and histories he occupies a small niche in the vanguard of the eighteenth century, along with Fontenelle. He is a "precursor," a kind of Voltaire *avant la lettre.*

In a way, this classification is justified, because his greatest influence was during the Enlightenment, and the *philosophes* did not hesitate to claim him as one of their own. The extent of their debt to him is only now being properly assessed.

Bayle cuts a rather awkward figure, moreover, in the stereotype of the seventeenth century which immediately recalls the classical age of French literature and the court nobility of Louis XIV. He never saw Versailles. He probably never saw a play of Racine, Corneille, or Molière or frequented the brilliant literary salons of Paris. He was a stranger to the gentility and polish of the world of Mme de Sévigné. His abundant, discursive prose was the antithesis of La Rochefoucauld's incisive and polished maxims.

But to see Bayle as an eighteenth-century *philosophe* born out of due time is necessarily to misunderstand both him and his age. His thought was molded by the forces of his seventeenth-century milieu, and it was addressed to his contemporaries.

The fact is that although Bayle was undeniably a seventeenth-century figure, his part of the French seventeenth century, that of the Reform, has hereto been relatively obscure and little studied. And he lived virtually all of his life within the confines of French Calvinism. He cast his lot with the "little flock," defended its interests, and spent almost half his life in exile because of his affiliation with it.

Three major studies of Bayle which have recently appeared should be sufficient to establish definitively the seventeenth-century character of Bayle and his writings. The most recent, *Essays on Pierre Bayle and Religious Controversy* by Walter Rex,[1] is a brilliant and thorough study of the Reformed Church in France from 1618 through 1700, its theology and apologists, its stresses and polemical tactics. It shows Bayle to be not only the point of departure for the Enlightenment but also the heir of a tradition of Calvinist rationalism and theological controversy. In doing so, Professor Rex links Bayle solidly with the Calvinist tradition and shows his thought to be the natural outgrowth of his Calvinist background. Recently the Protestant milieu has also been treated in breadth and depth by the late Professor Erich Haase in his *Einführung in die Literatur des Refuge.*[2]

The other two studies are the fruit of over ten years of research by Elizabeth Labrousse. The first, *Pierre Bayle: Du pays de Foix à la cité d'Erasme,* is now the standard life of Bayle and as a biography is in most respects definitive. The minutest details of his life and milieu have been researched and presented with thoroughness, insight, and critical acumen. This monumental work leaves no room for the traditional eighteenth-century image of a Bayle *philosophe.*

In her second volume, *Pierre Bayle: Hétérodoxie et rigorisme,*[3] Mme Labrousse undertakes an even more difficult task, that is, a systematic exposition of Bayle's thought. Now Bayle was an occasional writer, and never aspired to construct a philosophic system himself. In order to summarize his views on philosophic questions, one must winnow through the eight *in-folio* volumes which comprise his works, summarize and categorize his various pronouncements, and evaluate their relative importance. Perhaps such a work can never be more than approximate, but Madame Labrousse has given by far the best synthesis of Bayle's thought yet to appear. Her conclusion here likewise shows Bayle in the perspective of his predecessors and milieu.

I have not desired, therefore, to duplicate the work of any of these three studies by writing a biography of Bayle in the usual sense, or describing his thought in its encyclopedic vastness. Rather, drawing upon the contributions of each of them, I have taken another approach which might be helpful, and indeed necessary, in assessing the meaning and importance of Bayle's writings. What I have proposed is a chronological treatment of a limited but highly significant aspect of Bayle's thought, that is, his changing attitudes toward the relations of faith and reason. After analyzing Bayle's views on faith and reason as they appear in three major articles in the *Dictionnaire* (the most formal and systematic statement which they received), I have given a survey of critical opinion and then attempted to trace the development of his doctrine of faith from his early years until the time of the *Dictionnaire*. What emerges from this chronological approach is a somewhat different view than has usually been held of Pierre Bayle and his generation.

KARL C. SANDBERG

NOTES

1. Walter Rex, *Essays on Pierre Bayle and Religious Controversy* (La Haye, 1965).
2. Erich Haase, *Einführung in die Literatur des Refuge: Der Beitrag der französischen Protestanten zur Entwicklung analytischer Denkformen am Ende des 17. Jahrhunderts* (Berlin, 1959).
3. The first volume of Mme Labrousse's work appeared in 1963 and the second in 1964, under the sponsorship of the *International Archives of the History of Ideas* at the Hague. Professor Rex's *Essays* is also part of this same series.

1 Faith vs. The Manicheans and Pyrrhonians

THE least that can be said about the *Dictionnaire historique et critique* (1697)[1] is that it is one of the most unique documents in French letters and certainly one of the most impressive monuments of seventeenth-century erudition. Opening its pages at random one finds each article divided into text and notes, the former apparently serving only as a springboard for the latter. In the notes, there is a vast, disparate, and unsystematic assemblage of learning, the subjects having been chosen more from the author's interest than from their historical importance. Discussions, disquisitions, and digressions turn upon such varied subjects as geography, genealogies, the souls of animals, rabbinical speculation on the origin of the world, lives of Biblical heroes, obscure scholars of the sixteenth and seventeenth centuries, real and legendary figures of antiquity, and ecclesiastical disputes between Protestants, Catholics, heretics, and libertines. What is more surprising is that Bayle wrote its four massive, *in-folio* volumes single-handed in a little more than four years.

But what the reader immediately notices beyond the vastness of the erudition is the eminently critical tone of the *Dictionnaire*.

Historical error, first of all, is given no quarter. In the thousands of notes which comment on and explain the hundreds of articles, there are literally tens of thousands of references to document every point upon which there might be a question. Passages are cited in Greek and Latin in case the reader has doubts about the reading given. There is scarcely an article in which Bayle does not comment on or correct some error in the works of one of his predecessors or contemporaries. The *Grand Dictionnaire historique* of the abbot Louis Moréri, for example, first published in Lyons in 1674, had gone through seven editions by 1694, but swarmed with errors. Thus in Bayle's work one finds the notation that Moréri is mistaken three times here, five times there, that he has misquoted his sources, or that he has drawn faulty conclusions. Just as the maxims of La Rochefoucauld become screens to separate the true and the supposed motivations of the people, the *Dictionnaire* becomes a crucible in which the assertions and the commonplaces of seventeenth-century learning are proved and tested.

The *Dictionnaire* would nonetheless have remained only a work of erudition if its critical tone had not extended to more vital subjects. There is a trenchant moral criticism of certain Biblical personages who had long been thought to be saints and exemplars. Of these the article on David is the most famous, indicating that this "sun of holiness had his spots." Likewise, a repeated indictment of Christian intolerance runs through the four volumes. In the article "Japon," for example, Bayle makes the remark that modern Christian missionaries should not expect the proselyting success of the early Christians — in addition to whatever obstacle the hidden designs of Providence might pose to the foreign missions, early Christianity was mild and peace-loving, whereas modern Christianity has become a religion of blood and the sword. It is not unreasonable to imagine that in the libraries of the *philosophes* such passages were thumbworn.

Of even more significance, however, was the critique of faith and reason in the famous articles "Pyrrhon," "Manichéens," and "Pauliciens." Here the limitations and debility of speculative reason were set forth much in the manner of Kant, but only after a penetrating description of the terrible objections reason could raise to Christian theology.

By "faith," Bayle meant belief in the basic Calvinist doctrines, based on the authority of revelation, and the mysteries common to Catholics and Protestants. By "reason," he meant belief based upon the critical Cartesian method, which insisted on clarity and evidence as the standards of truth.

In the article "Pyrrhon," Bayle imagined a dialogue between two abbots, the first of whom maintained disdainfully that it was unthinkable that there could be any Pyrrhonians in the modern day when the darkness of pagan philosophy had been dispelled by the revealed light of the Gospel. The second abbot, who was a "bon philosophe," replied that if Arcesilas came back to the world and undertook to combat our theologians, he would be a thousand times more dangerous than he was for the dogmatists of ancient Greece (note B, p. 2306).

In order to hope for a victory over a skeptic, the second abbot continued, it is necessary to establish a *criterium veritatis,* that is, certain marks by which the truth is universally recognizable, but from the Christian position this is impossible. It is useless to try to prove the truth of Christianity to a skeptic by invoking the criterium of self-evident propositions, because the skeptic would immediately point out that the most evident propositions contradict the dogmas of Christianity. For example, it is evident that two things which do not differ from a third are not different from one another and that there is no difference between individuality, nature, and personality, and yet the mystery of the Trinity contradicts these two propositions. It is morally evident that one should prevent evil if possible, that it is a sin to permit evil if one can prevent it, and that a creature which did not exist at the time an evil action was committed cannot justly be punished as an accomplice to this action; and yet the doctrine of Original Sin contradicts these maxims. Now if one makes exceptions to the most evident propositions that reason can formulate, on the basis that man's ways are not God's ways, he abandons any hope of ever establishing a rational *criterium veritatis,* and the victory goes to the Pyrrhonian. The second abbot therefore concluded that one must not lightly undertake to debate with Pyrrhonians, for it is a mistake to think that their sophistry can be easily unmasked by unaided reason. To the contrary, one must first of all make them feel the infirmity of reason in order that this feeling may bring them to the better guide, which is faith (note B, p. 2307).

It is a drastic remedy and one fraught with consequence, as Montaigne observed, to disarm oneself in order to disarm one's enemy. Bayle still did not hesitate to abase reason in order to save faith. The reasoning of Sextus Empiricus, the greatest subtlety of which the human mind is capable, because it precluded any conclusion, was for Bayle only an evidence of the infirmity of reason. Reason, which should guide into certainty, ended up by asking us to doubt whether or not we should doubt, and the checkmate of the intellect caused the great reasoner to exclaim:

> Quel chaos, quelle gêne pour l'esprit! Il semble donc que ce malheureux état est le plus propre de tous à nous convaincre que notre raison est une voie d'égarement, puisque lorsqu'elle se déploie avec le plus de subtilité, elle nous jette dans un tel abîme. La suite naturelle de cela doit être de renoncer à ce guide, et d'en demander un meilleur à la cause de toutes choses. C'est un grand pas vers la religion chrétienne; car elle veut . . . que nous captivions notre entendement à l'obéissance de la foi.

Bayle then cited Pascal and Calvin, who had said essentially the same thing (note C, p. 2308).

The theme was again treated in the articles on the Manicheans and the Paulicians. Here Bayle maintained (1) that no sect or system, orthodox Christianity included, could offer a satisfactory rational explanation of the origin of evil; (2) that these heretics could raise insurmountable philosophic (rational) objections to Christian doctrines; and (3) that reason itself, being incapable of dealing with this problem, must be subjected to faith.

It is true, stated Bayle in the article "Manichéens," that Christianity could best the Manicheans by *a priori* reasoning; the clearest and most certain ideas dictated by the order and the harmony of the universe persuade us that a necessary, eternal, and self-existent Being must also be omnipotent, infinite, and endowed with all perfections. However, *a priori* reasoning is shipwrecked on the inexplicable fact of evil, for one of the necessary conditions of a good system is that it can explain the facts.

The fact is that although the heavens and the earth proclaim the glory and unity of God, man is an enigma. He is wicked and miserable — his history is little more than an account of crimes and misfortunes. But on the other hand, there are outstanding examples of goodness and virtue in humanity, and this dichotomy of good and evil is best explained by the Manicheans and their doctrine of two opposing and co-eternal principles. Bayle has Zoroaster say that ". . . puisque le principal caractère d'un bon système est d'être capable de donner raison des expériences, et que la seule incapacité de les expliquer est une preuve qu'une hypothèse n'est pas bonne, quelque belle qu'elle paraisse d'ailleurs, demeurez d'accord que je frappe au but en admettant deux principes et vous n'y frappez pas, vous qui n'en admettez qu'un seul" (note D, p. 1899).

But Bayle does not give the victory to the Manichean reasoner, whose doctrine of the two eternal Beings disputing the dominion of the universe is also unsatisfactory because it leads into the most dreadful immorality (note B, 1897). And he declares that in addition ". . . ces hérétiques s'embarassaient puérilement lorsqu'ils descendaient dans le détail" (note D, p. 1900). The conclusion is that reason is too weak to unravel the mystery:

> La raison humaine est trop faible pour cela; c'est un principe de destruction et non pas d'édification: elle n'est propre qu'à former des doutes et à tourner à droite et à gauche pour éterniser une dispute . . . [La raison] n'est propre qu'à faire connaître à l'homme ses ténèbres et son impuissance, et la nécessité d'une autre révélation [que la révélation naturelle de la raison]. C'est celle de l'Ecriture. C'est là que nous trouvons de quoi réfuter invinciblement l'hypothèse des deux principes.

Thus, since the authority of the Scripture is the only effective arm against Manichean dualism, the Christian theologian would do well not to dispute with a Manichean philosopher on purely philosophic grounds (note D, p. 1900).

In the article "Pauliciens," Bayle enlarged upon the theme of evil and concluded that the Christian theologians could not give an explanation of it without exposing themselves to overwhelming difficulties. It is just as ridiculous, he argued, to say that God permitted man to sin in order to show His goodness in redeeming man from sin as it is to imagine a father who would break the legs of his children in order to show his goodness in resetting the bones. It does not help to say that God permitted man to sin so as not to take away man's freedom of choice. Who would not blame a mother who, knowing that her daughter would be seduced at a ball, did not prevent her from going to the ball? It does not help to say that the Devil is the author of sin, because the only alternative to saying that God is the author of the Devil and hence of sin, is to say that the Devil is co-eternal with God and thus to concede the dispute to the Manichean.

Reason, then, dictates the necessity, philosophically, of a benevolent and omnipotent First Cause, but the fact of evil contradicts the findings of reason, again giving Bayle the occasion to remark upon the debility of man's intellect: "Qui n'admirera et qui ne déplorera la destinée de notre raison? Voilà les manichéens qui, avec une hypothèse tout à fait absurde et contradictoire, expliquent les expériences cent fois mieux que ne font les orthodoxes avec la supposition si juste, si nécessaire, si uniquement véritable d'un premier principe infiniment bon et tout puissant" (note E, p. 2205). On the basis of this antinomy, Bayle once more concluded that reason had met with defeat, and he therefore held that "il faut humblement reconnaître que toute la philosophie est ici à bout et que sa faiblesse nous doit conduire aux lumières de la révélation, où nous trouverons l'ancre sûre et ferme" (note H, p, 2210).

These articles scandalized certain of Bayle's fellow Protestant refugees. At the request of the Walloon Consistory of Rotterdam, Bayle wrote some explanatory articles for the second edition of the *Dictionnaire* (1702). He only intensified his position, not only insisting on the disparity of faith and reason, but also forcing a choice between them.

The doctrines of the orthodox faith are above reason, Bayle explained. They cannot be understood by reason and therefore can be neither proved nor disproved by reason. Furthermore, they were never intended as objects of knowledge, but rather as objects of faith. Christ never gave a commandment to dispute or argue but only to believe. St. Paul declared the wisdom of men anathema, saying that the true Christian should walk by faith and not by sight, and this should be enough to convince anyone that it is useless to dispute about the mysteries. The reason for these commandments, continued Bayle, is seen in the nature of faith and knowledge, for the faith of a Christian produces a complete persuasion while its object remains inevident. The knowledge of the philosopher on the other hand, is accompanied by both clarity and complete certainty. "Si donc un chrétien entreprenait de soutenir contre un philosophe le mystere de la Trinité, il opposerait à des objections évidentes un objet inévident. Ne serait-ce point se battre les yeux bandés et les mains liées, et avoir pour antagoniste un homme qui se peut servir de toutes ses facultés?"

Because the nature of faith is so different from that of reason, Bayle declared, one must necessarily choose between philosophy and the Gospel. If one wishes to believe only what is clear, evident, and confirmed by natural ideas, one should take philosophy and leave Christianity. If one wishes to believe the incomprehensible mysteries of religion, one should take Christianity and leave philosophy. For to possess the evident and the incomprehensible at the same time is manifestly impossible.

He maintained, however, that the unbelievers and pagans could draw no advantage from this avowal of incomprehensibility because the same reason which raised objections to the Christian system could raise objections to the pagan systems. Reason is capable of inventing difficulties but incapable of finding their solution (*EclP*, p. 3006). If a Christian really understood the nature of faith and reason, he continued, he would neither enter into vain disputations and wranglings nor take alarm at any rational objection which his opponent might raise, for

> la foi mettra [le véritable chrétien] au dessus des régions où règnent les tempètes de la dispute. Il se verra dans un poste d'où il entendra gronder au dessous de lui le tonnerre des arguments et des *distinguo*, et n'en sera point ébranlé. Poste ... d'où il verra dans une parfaite tranquillité les faiblesses de la raison et l'égarement des mortels qui ne suivent que ce guide. Tout chrétien qui se laisse déconcerter par les objections des incrédules, et qui en reçoit du scandale, a un pied dans la même fosse qu'eux" (*EclP*, p. 3004).

In short, reason can raise insurmountable objections to the Christian dogmas, but reason itself is a deceptive and fallible guide. All it can do is to lead one to the fortress of revelation and faith, which is the last resource of the Christian. The Christian's duty is not to argue but to believe and be still.

Bayle stated that his motives in reporting all of the philosophic difficulties surrounding orthodox Christianity were (1) to fulfill his duty as an historian, who must record both the *pro* and the *con* (*EclP,* p. 3004), (2) to combat incidentally the Socinian emphasis on reason (*EclP,* p. 2986), and (3) to make his readers understand the nature of faith, which is to accept revealed truths for no other reason than to obey God. Those who believe because of philosophic reasons have no part in faith, for the merit of faith becomes greater as its object becomes more incomprehensible and requires a greater sacrifice in order to submit oneself to God. Now most readers, Bayle continued, are so indolent that they need to be prodded on to examine the nature of their faith by long lists of the difficulties which surround the Christian religion, and those who are unaware of the force of these philosophic observations are also unaware of what they owe to the Almighty.[2]

This doctrine is essentially a fideism, old in Christianity and on the surface innocuous, but of great consequence in the hands of rationalists for whom any fideism is impossible. And the explanations raise more questions than they answer. Taken at his word, Bayle was a believing and conservative Protestant when he wrote the *Dictionnaire.* But can he be taken at his word? Can one who insists on compiling long lists of terrible difficulties attending faith really be among the faithful? Even though Bayle clearly abases reason, how can one who so strips away the rational supports of faith and so forcefully states all of the rational difficulties attending faith intend anything but the undermining and destruction of faith? And if Bayle was sincere, what brought such a cogent reasoner to abase reason?

Before seeking the answers to these questions in Bayle's life and writings, it will be helpful to see what reaction he has provoked, from the eighteenth century to the present.

NOTES

1. The edition cited in this work (unless otherwise indicated) is the third edition, published in Rotterdam in 1720. It will be referred to as *DHC.* For abbreviations of other of Bayle's works, see the "List of Abbreviations" preceding the Bibliography. In all quotations the spelling has been modernized.

2. Bayle's doctrine of faith is ably discussed by Richard Popkin in "Pierre Bayle's Place in 17th-Century Scepticism," in *Pierre Bayle, le philosophe de Rotterdam,* ed. Paul Dibon, Amsterdam, 1959.

2 Bayle and the Critics

DURING the bitterly fought contest between the *philosophes* and the Church party in the eighteenth century, the orthodox found Bayle's writings on faith and reason somewhat less than edifying. True, Bayle had always protested that he was an orthodox Christian and had presented his views on faith and reason as a kind of defense of faith. The defenders of the faith nonetheless felt that his arguments supported Christianity as a rope supports a hanged man. Far from being a genuine believer, in the eyes of the Church party, Bayle was a skeptic, an atheist, or worse (if worse there might be).

In 1752, for example, Philippe-Louis Joly, an abbot of the Roman Church, made a summary of all the answers to Bayle up to that time.[1] A few citations are illustrative of the kind of reaction that the Huguenot refugee provoked.

Even though Bayle always protested the purest orthodoxy and virtue, said one writer, he worked for forty years to compile in one work a whole library of irreligion and infamy.[2] He turned the best arguments for faith into sophistry, said another, never missing a chance to raise doubt about Providence or the immortality of the soul. Worse still, he submitted the oracles of the Scripture to his own judgment, destroying their authority, and in his pride and unbelief, declared war on God Himself.[3]

Joly himself shared this opinion and declared that

> cet auteur dont la fantaisie était d'établir le pyrrhonisme et d'inspirer aux hommes de l'éloignement pour la raison savait bien que son *Dictionnaire* serait lu par une infinité de gens qui ne seraient point accoutumés à réfléchir et qui loin d'avoir des principes solides sur les sciences n'en auraient même aucune teinture. . . . Il n'ignorait pas que le joug de la religion pèse à bien des coeurs qui seraient charmés de lire ce qui va à en décharger en le dépouillant de certitude (I, x-xi).

Not less vehement was Jean-Pierre de Crousaz, a Swiss mathematician who undertook to answer all of the objections to Christianity that the *philosophe* party found in Bayle's writings. He likewise felt that Bayle had intended to exempt no religious belief when he separated faith and reason. How could it be otherwise when some reflections in the *Dictionnaire* fill the mind with doubt and make it despair of finding truth; when others set faith and reason in contradiction; when others maintain that one can just as easily believe in the most absurd and irreligious systems as in a most holy and righteous God?[4]

The same effect which de Crousaz deplored, Voltaire recognized and applauded. One of the few things upon which the two probably agreed was that Bayle was not among the believers, as is suggested by Voltaire's appreciation of Bayle:

> Ses plus grands ennemis sont forcés d'avouer qu'il n'y a pas une seule ligne dans ses ouvrages qui soit un blasphème évident contre la religion chrétienne; mais ses plus grands défenseurs avouent que dans les articles de controverse il n'y a pas une seule page qui ne conduise le lecteur au doute et souvent à l'incrédulité. On ne pouvait le convaincre d'être impie; mais il faisait des impies en mettant les objections contre nos dogmes dans un jour si lumineux, qu'il n'était pas possible à une foi médiocre de n'être pas ébranlée; et malheureusement la plus grande partie de ses lecteurs n'a qu'une foi très-médiocre.[5]

All of the *philosophes,* as a matter of fact, claimed Bayle as one of their own. Read in their milieu, his affirmations of orthodoxy were shifts and dodges to which they themselves had to resort; and to them such a subtle and powerful reasoner could not be serious in discounting the powers of reason. They borrowed his rational critique of the Church and its theology, transformed it according to the needs of the moment, and discounted his critique of reason and its attendant fideism. In the words of Paul Hazard:

> Bayle n'a point cessé d'agir. C'était faire oeuvre pie que le réfuter: il était mort depuis un demi-siècle, depuis trois quarts de siècle, qu'on s'acharnait encore contre lui, ainsi qu'au premier jour: tant il continuait d'apparaître au premier rang des sceptiques. En fait, son *Dictionnaire* figurait à la place d'honneur dans les bibliothèques; on le rééditait, on le traduisait; soit qu'il s'enflât d'édition en édition, soit qu'on le réduisît en extraits, ou analyses, il était toujours l'arsenal où toutes les armes étaient puisées quand il s'agissait de remplacer l'autorité par la critique.[6]

The nineteenth-century writings on Bayle were, with few exceptions, based upon the eighteenth-century view of him. And since the broad issues of faith and reason were still very much alive, Bayle was still a controversial figure. Many studies were undertaken to attack or defend him, but seldom to understand him.

Those who spoke from a conservative position generally considered him to be a skeptic but differed substantially on the nature and intent of his skepticism. Sayous, for example, writing in 1853, held that Bayle was principally a skeptic and critic who divorced faith and reason only out of love of paradox and contradiction and thus undermined the faith of his contemporaries.[7] On the other hand, Charles Lenient, a Catholic and the most influential Bayle critic of the nineteenth century, maintained in his Sorbonne thesis of 1855 that Bayle introduced skepticism only in order to establish tolerance. Accepting Voltaire's evaluation, Lenient saw in Bayle a desire to rid society of the credulity, pride, stubbornness, despotism, and intolerance which result from convictions held too strongly or defended too ardently. To accomplish this purpose, said Lenient, Bayle undertook to destroy these convictions by "la guerre faite à l'absolu. . . ."[8]

Some twenty years after Lenient's study appeared, Arsène Deschamps, a Belgian philosopher anxious to counteract Bayle's contribution to the "modern malady of unbelief," advanced yet another interpretation of the latter's skepticism: because Bayle had failed to acquire any sound philosophic principles during his youth, he lacked the means of interpreting the mass of learning resulting from his voracious reading. It was for this reason that Bayle denied the possibility of ever reaching a conclusion and forming the convictions that Deschamps felt to be so necessary.[9]

Ferdinand Brunetière, however, wrote at the end of the nineteenth century that Bayle ended up an atheist, after first passing through the progressive stages of Socianism and deism. His conclusion was based upon Bayle's insistence on the disparity between faith and reason,[10] and his contemporary, Emile Faguet, concurred. Faguet, like others before him, found it incomprehensible that the great reasoner could have been sincere in subjecting reason to faith, arguing that "son athéisme, qui est incontestable . . . consiste à affirmer qu'il ne faut pas s'adresser à la raison pour croire en Dieu . . . [et] que pour lui, Bayle, qui ne sait que raisonner, il ne peut point, en conscience, nous promettre de nous conduire à la croyance. . . ."[11]

Similarly, the commentators who studied the Rotterdam philosopher from a liberal or anti-religious position also saw in him an apologist for reason, but they defended what the orthodox had condemned. There was nonetheless a great divergence between their views. One of the lesser of these critics, Cazes, published an essay on Bayle as part of the polemics that a group of liberals was carrying on with the Bishop of Pamiers in 1905. In the essay he pictured Bayle as wielding the sword of reason against all forms of religion and asserted that: "... entre la raison qui affirme et la foi qui nie, il faut se décider. C'est pour la raison que Bayle se prononce. . . . Voilà comment Bayle est amené, au long de sa laborieuse carrière, à engager une lutte gigantesque contre toutes les métaphysiques et toutes les religions."[12]

Up until this time (*ca.* 1905), most critics, whether liberal or conservative, had seen only a negative or destructive element in the writings of the great skeptic (or atheist). Jean Delvolvé who in 1906 published the most important and comprehensive study of Bayle up to that date, was the first to emphasize a positive value in Bayle's thought. A recent commentator, Paul Dibon, gives the following evaluation of Delvolvé:

> ... il porta un coup définitif à la conception toute négative qu'on s'était faite communément jusqu'alors de Bayle. . . . Sans nier tout ce qui chez son auteur prépare l'oeuvre critique du XVIIIe siècle, il s'attacha à mettre en évidence l'apport positif de la pensée de Bayle dans l'histoire des idées. Il montra que, derrière les apparences négatives et la forme non systématique, une méthode est en action . . . que Delvolvé croit devoir . . . caractériser comme un "empirisme positiviste."[13]

Delvolvé nonetheless held that Bayle was a militant opponent of all religion, declaring that "autant il se tient exactement à la lettre des dogmes [de l'orthodoxie calviniste], autant il est certain qu'il en est aussi dégagé, et aussi ennemi qu'il est possible de l'être."[14] And Delvolvé elsewhere stated that "son rationalisme est étranger et opposé à toute métaphysique religieuse, si humble soit-elle dans ses prétentions, appauvrie jusqu'au plus vague déisme."[15]

Edmond Lacoste, a Belgian scholar who in 1926 published a very thorough analysis of the contents of Bayle's journal, *Les Nouvelles de la République des Lettres,* felt that Delvolvé's synthesis of Bayle's system was definitive. He also concluded that Bayle was leading the attack on traditional theology and religion, for, according to Lacoste, Bayle's intent was to abolish all dogmas by undermining the authority of revelation and tradition and shearing religion of everything except morality.[16]

The first major study of Bayle produced in the United States was *Bayle the Sceptic* (1931) by Howard Robinson. It has been one of the most popular books on Bayle, but in spite of the title, the author seemed uncertain whether to classify Bayle as an atheist or skeptic. For him, "Bayle had such an invincible antipathy to theological and philosophical dogmatizers that it is more reasonable to think of him not as an atheist, but as a sceptic. Yet one cannot be certain, for he was at least the equal of Spinoza in his 'shifts and equivocations.'"[17] In any event, Robinson considered Bayle a rationalist and unbeliever because ". . . his mind was incapable of submitting to the authority of faith."[18]

But if Bayle were really such an unbeliever why did he remain within the Reformed Church all his life? Paul Hazard opined that Bayle indeed came to repudiate everything which was incompatible with reason, but he claimed to remain a believer in order to attack the doctrines of religion more effectively. "Bayle prétend ne pas attaquer la croyance comme telle," said Hazard, "il se donne même l'air de la respecter; il ne fait que suivre et que répéter, dit-il, les arguments de ceux qui la défendent: n'avouent-ils point qu'il y a dans toute religion un mystère initial? C'est cela même, un mystère incompatible avec la raison. . . . Plus que jamais, il se place dans la forteresse pour l'ébranler; au milieu de ses défenseurs, pour jeter le trouble parmi eux."[19]

And a variation of the theme of an anti-religious Bayle is in the work of Rateni, a recent Italian critic, who depicts him as a libertine.[20]

But what was overlooked both by the attackers and by the defenders of this elusive thinker is that there are, in reality, two Bayles — the one who existed in the minds of the eighteenth and nineteenth centuries and who continued to act and change form from critic to critic and the other who lived and moved in seventeenth-century France and Holland. If Bayle is read in the context of the Enlightenment, his professed fideism is an anachronism and the only possible effect of the articles "Pyrrhon," "Manichéens," and "Pauliciens," is to exalt reason and abase faith.

If one places Bayle in the seventeenth century and takes him more or less at his word, his fideism is possible. In the century of Sir Thomas Browne and his *Religio medici* his doctrine of faith can find company. In Pascal's reasons of the heart which reason does not know it can even find respectability. Nor should one forget that Bayle was a contemporary of John Dryden who could also end his religious quest by bowing before the incomprehensible and saying

> Good life, be now my task, my doubts are done
> (What more could fright my faith than three-in-one?)
> ("The Hind and The Panther." Lines 78–79).

A line of critics starting with Sainte-Beuve did not discount Bayle's sincerity in his professions of faith and tended therefore to place him somehow among the believers. "Bayle était religieux," said Sainte-Beuve, "et nous tirons cette conclusion moins de ce qu'il communiait quatre fois l'an, de ce qu'il assistait aux prières publiques et aux sermons, que de plusieurs sentiments de résignation et de confiance en Dieu qu'il manifesta dans ces lettres. . . ."[21]

Another of the few nineteenth-century commentators to see Bayle as a Protestant was another Protestant, Emile Jeanmaire, who in 1862 did a thesis on Bayle for the Protestant seminary at Strasbourg. His conclusion was that although Bayle did not believe everything in the Confession of Faith, he nonetheless remained loyally within the Reformed Church — he may have had an irreligious mind, suggested Jeanmaire, but his heart remained religious.[22]

The publication in 1905 and 1906 of the studies by Cazes and Delvolvé provoked a reaction on the part of Schoell, a Protestant critic, who maintained that Bayle was not anti-religious but, if anything, anti-rationalist. Bayle was not intent on destroying religious belief as such, but aimed instead at human pride which in his day was most often manifest in the form of religion. Notwithstanding Bayle's attacks on "religionists," Schoell still felt that he chose to remain within the Protestant fold, as a tolerant, liberal Protestant emancipated from dogma and ritual, preferring to live with doubt than to make the leap of faith.[23]

Four years later — in 1912 — Cornelia Serrurier, a Dutch historian, did the first study of Bayle in his Rotterdam milieu. She emphasized the genuinely religious element in his works, repudiating the picture of the "sceptique railleur" created by tradition and of the "positiviste libéré" created by Delvolvé. Where is there any logic or unity in Bayle's thought, she asked, unless he is placed among the believers? However, Bayle was not principally a philosopher, according to her, but rather a pessimistic moralist.[24]

More probing into Bayle's early life yielded a similar conclusion. In 1939 Ruth Cowdrick did a Columbia University thesis on Bayle's early reading and its effect upon his intellectual development up to 1684. Although Miss Cowdrick assumed, without studying the question, that Bayle eventually lost his religious faith, she concluded on the basis of her analysis of his early correspondence that he had not done so by 1684. She did not believe that he was still entirely orthodox, having adopted an attitude similar to that of the Christian deists, but she strongly affirmed that up to that date he had retained the essentials of the Christian faith.[25]

The private life and the correspondence of Bayle all show a completely different man than is revealed in his published works — this was the conclusion of Annie Barnes, who maintained that he was indeed a sincere Protestant although he lived in unconscious contradiction with his religion.[26]

Or does Bayle's printed work really show him to be so irreligious? Perhaps the critics have failed to give due weight to all aspects of his

thought. Paul André, a modern Catholic author, advanced the thesis
that Bayle has been misinterpreted because "après tant de morceaux
où il accumulait voluptueusement les difficultés que la raison oppose
à la foi, on a pris pour une feinte ceux où il indique sèchement les
ressources de la foi contre la raison." For André, the seeming disparity
in Bayle's thought is simply the result of "le vieux, l'éternel dualisme
humain entre la pensée qui se formule et la pensée en lutte avec
l'inconnaissable."[27]

Another significant essay on Bayle is that of Professor W. H.
Barber, who maintains that the familiar eighteenth-century view
which associates Bayle with the Age of Reason does not give a true
picture of Bayle's thought and intentions and that one cannot explain
Bayle's life without accepting his profession of faith as genuine.
Moreover, he continues ". . . it is important to emphasize that Bayle's
whole conception of the character of man and of human history is
not only profoundly Christian but essentially Calvinist." Taking Bayle's
writings at their face value, he states that Bayle believed in the
efficaciousness of grace and that he held that "true religious belief
cannot be the result of any rational process on the part of the individual, but only the effect of the divine and mysterious illumination
of the human conscience." The basis of Bayle's thought then is a
profound fideism: there is more value in believing a doctrine because
it is revealed than in believing it because reason dictates it.[28]

Thus far, a survey of Bayle studies has yielded only diversity.
The philosopher who spent his life in study and intellectual contest
was a skeptic, a rationalist, a Socinian, an atheist, a deist, a libertine,
or a positivist, unless he was a moralist, a freethinking Protestant, a
nominal Protestant, or a fideist. The view one holds of him is con-
tingent upon the milieu in which he is placed. The direction suggested
by Professor Barber was the one to be further explored, and in 1959
appeared a landmark in Bayle studies, a collection of essays entitled
Pierre Bayle, le philosophe de Rotterdam, under the editorship of
Paul Dibon. These essays discussed Bayle in relationship to the
philosophical currents of the seventeenth century, filled in biographical
information, and in general insisted that he was to be seen truly only
in his own age and milieu. It remained for the monumental studies of
Mme Labrousse to identify Bayle definitively with the Reform and for
Professor Rex's thorough, solid treatment of seventeenth-century con-
troversy[30] to show Bayle's writings to be a part of the current of
Calvinist rationalism.

But even so, two questions are still unresolved. What permits
one to assume that the doctrine of faith in the *Dictionnaire* is the

genuine expression of Bayle's real views? If he was sincere, what lead one of the most cogent and persistent reasoners to choose faith over reason?

My own view is that in the *Dictionnaire* Bayle was giving free and authentic expression to conclusions grounded in his religious and intellectual formation and molded by his participation in the Catholic-Protestant controversies of 1682–87. But the expression of his belief in the *Dictionnaire* was more than doctrinal — it was also polemical, occasioned by and directed toward individuals within his immediate environment. The Rotterdam philosopher indeed helped to prepare the Enlightenment, but it is difficult to believe that he foresaw or that he intended that his influence should yield the results it did.

The question of his sincerity will be dealt with in Chapter 10 after his changing attitudes toward the issues of faith and reason have been traced from his childhood through the *Dictionnaire*.

NOTES

1. Joly, *Remarques critiques sur le "Dictionnaire" de Bayle* (Paris, 1752), I, 1–50.

2. *Essai sur le beau,* p. 197, no author nor date, cited by Joly, I, xiv.

3. *Essais sur les philosophes, ou les égarements de la raison sans la foi,* in *Bibliothèque française,* pt. II, art. I, p. 185, no place nor date, cited by Joly, I, xv.

4. De Crousaz, *Examen du pyrrhonisme ancien et moderne* (La Haye, 1733), p. 201. An answer to this work was given in the Preface of the *Nouvelles Lettres de Bayle,* 2 vols. (La Haye, 1739).

5. Voltaire, "Lettres sur Rabelais et sur d'autres auteurs accusés d'avoir mal parlé de la religion chrétienne," in *Oeuvres complètes de Voltaire,* ed. Louis Moland (Paris, 1877–1885), xxvi, 502.

6. *La Pensée européenne au XVIIIème siècle de Montesquieu à Lessing* (Paris [1946]), I, 44. There are two other major studies of Bayle's influence on eighteenth-century thought and literature. The first is C. Louise Thijssen-Schouten's essay: "La Diffusion européenne des idées de Bayle," in *Pierre Bayle, le philosophe de Rotterdam* (Amsterdam, 1959), pp. 150–195. The second is by Professor Howard Robinson in his work *Bayle the Sceptic* (New York, 1931), pp. 246–309. Several other critics have treated the same subject but with less detail and precision. See Ferdinand Brunetière, "La Critique de Bayle," in *Etudes critiques sur l'histoire de la littérature française,* 2nd ed., 5th Ser. (Paris, 1896), Vol. V, pp. 165–174; Jean Delvolvé, *Essai sur Pierre Bayle, religion critique et philosophie positive* (Paris, 1906), pp. 425–431; Horatio E. Smith, *The Literary Criticism of Pierre Bayle* (Albany, 1912), pp. 126–132; Edmond Lacoste, *Bayle, nouvelliste et critique littéraire* (Paris, 1929), pp. 242–258. The work of Richard Popkin in the history of skepticism frequently points up the influence which Bayle had upon the skeptics of the Enlightenment. See "Scepticism in the Enlightenment," in *Studies on Voltaire and the Eighteenth Century,* XXIV–XXVII (1963), 1327–1333.

7. A. Sayous, *Histoire de la littérature française à l'étranger depuis le commencement du XVIIe siècle* (Paris, 1853), I, 365–366.

8. See Charles Lenient, *Etude sur Bayle* (Paris, 1855), p. 21.

9. Deschamps, *La Genèse du scepticisme érudit chez Bayle* (Liège, 1878), p. 22.

10. Brunetière, "La Critique de Bayle," *Etudes critiques sur l'histoire de la littérature française*, 2nd ed., 5th series (Paris, 1896), pp. 111–112.

11. Faguet, *Dixhuitième Siècle* in *Etudes littéraires* (Paris, 1890), p. 15.

12. *Pierre Bayle, sa vie, ses idées, son influence, son oeuvre* (Paris, 1905), pp. 42–43. Cazes borrowed extensively from Lenient. See Horatio E. Smith, "Bayle and his Biographers," *Modern Language Notes*, XXVII (1912), 158–159.

13. Dibon, "Redécouverte de Bayle," in *Pierre Bayle, le philosophe de Rotterdam* (Amsterdam, 1959), pp. ix–x.

14. Delvolvé, *Essai sur Pierre Bayle, religion critique et philosophie positiviste* (Paris, 1906), p. 336.

15. Delvolvé, *Essai*, p. 140. See also p. 346.

16. Lacoste, *Bayle nouvelliste et critique littéraire* (Paris, 1929), p. 183, note.

17. Robinson, *Bayle the Sceptic* (New York, 1931), p. 218.

18. Robinson, *Bayle the Sceptic,* p. 215.

19. Hazard, *La Crise de la conscience européenne* [2nd ed.] (Paris, 1961), I, 100.

20. Benito Rateni, "L'Interpretazione critica del Bayle alla luce degli studi piu recenti," *Rassegna di filosofia*, I (1952), 242.

21. Sainte-Beuve, "Du génie critique de Bayle," in *Portraits littéraires* (Paris [1843]), I, 377–378.

22. Jeanmaire, *Essai sur la critique religieuse de Pierre Bayle* (Strasbourg, 1862), p. 99.

23. T. Schoell, "Pierre Bayle, à propos de deux livres récents (Delvolvé et Cazes) avec quelques notes bibliographiques," *Bulletin de la Société de l'histoire du protestantisme français*, LVIII (1908), 363.

24. Serrurier, *Pierre Bayle en Hollande* (Lausanne, 1912), pp. 207–208.

25. Cowdrick, *The Early Reading of Pierre Bayle* (Scottdale, Pa., 1939), pp. 156–157.

26. Barnes, *Jean Le Clerc et les "Nouvelles de la République des Lettres"* (Paris, 1938), p. 236.

27. André, *La Jeunesse de Bayle, tribun de la tolérance* (Genève [1953]), 16–17.

28. Barber, "Pierre Bayle: Faith and Reason," in *The French Mind* (Oxford, 1952), pp. 117–118.

29. Labrousse, *Pierre Bayle* (La Haye, 1963–64), vols. I and II.

30. Rex, *Essays on Pierre Bayle and Religious Controversy* (La Haye, 1965). Two recent articles — E. D. James, "Scepticism and Fideism in Bayle's *Dictionnaire*," *French Studies*, XVI (1962), 308–323, and H. T. Mason, "Pierre Bayle's Religious Views," *French Studies*, XVII (1963), 205–217 — present a dissenting view from the recent trend. Prof. James sees Bayle as fideistic toward proof of the immortality of the soul, free will, and the controlling activity of a benevolent Providence, but not toward the Scriptures, which Bayle supposedly felt to be rationally demonstrable, and toward natural law, and the existence of God. (p. 318) What remained after Bayle's critique of Christianity was something similar to the beliefs and attitudes of the deists. According to Professor Mason, Bayle's final attitude was one of skepticism (a kind of wandering in the void without reference to any stable point), not fideism, which takes God, and what the idea of God entails, as a point of reference without any rational or human support for one's act of belief. In his skepticism, Bayle attacked Christianity, howbeit obliquely, and in disguise. (p. 215) These two studies appeared before the books by Mme Labrousse and Professor Rex, which are much more complete and which answer the objections raised, though not directly. For the question of Bayle's attitudes toward the Scripture, see *infra* Chapter 6. The question of his sincerity is discussed *infra* Chapter 10.

3   The Roots of Faith

On September 2, 1670, young Pierre, then twenty-three, ended a two-week ride by entering the free city of Geneva. He planned to attend the Protestant Academy and counted on the sale of his horse to buy him new clothes and get him established. The horse brought him only two *écus*. Whether the horse market was slow or whether in his inexperience he sold his horse à la Gil Blas, it was not the first time that he had miscalculated.

Less than two years before, he had gone to study logic and philosophy at the Jesuit Academy of Toulouse, and being persuaded by a "subtle polemicist" that his Protestant ways were in error, he had converted to Catholicism. During the next eighteen months he decided that his move had been precipitous, being based on specious reasoning, and on August 19, 1670, he abjured his Catholicism and returned to the Protestant fold.

His reconversion was costly. In order to escape the penalties decreed for such "relapsed" heretics, he was obliged to leave his home country (he was never to return to Southern France or to see his family again) and seek some position outside of the realms of Louis XIV. He had decided to go to Geneva where he would prepare himself for the Reformed ministry.[1]

His reconversion to the Reform was also one of the milestones of his religious life,[2] and much of the misreading of Bayle's later writings stems from the failure to properly assess its nature and importance.

Several critics have held that the effect of Bayle's double conversion was to destroy or seriously weaken his faith. He changed religions with as little concern as one changes books, said Lenient, whose opinion was almost universally accepted during the nineteenth century. It was without any inner struggle and left only an incurable skepticism.[3] Deschamps shared the opinion — Bayle's conversions showed only that the force of one's convictions is not a sign of their truth and that the evidence *pro* and *con* can appear equally probable.[4] Delvolvé was even more categorical, stating that "Bayle en quittant Toulouse n'est plus un homme de foi."[5]

These conclusions, however, seem to misjudge the entire tenor of Bayle's education and early milieu, an omission all the more important because Bayle later attributed his return to the Reform to the impressions of childhood which had "regained the ascendancy." What were these impressions? What was the soil that had nourished and rooted Bayle's faith during the first twenty-three years of his life?

It was the soil of the French Reform with its paradoxical traditions of isolationism and openness, rationalism and subjectivity, grace and works. These inherently incompatible elements co-existed peacefully, and Bayle unconsciously drew his early thought and attitudes from them. It was the interplay of these forces which took Bayle into the Catholic confession, brought him back to the religion of his fathers, and rooted him in the Reform for the rest of his life.

The culture into which Bayle was born was isolated geographically. His birthplace, the town of Carla in the present department of Arriège, was one of the poorest places in one of the poorest provinces of France, removed from the mainstream of commerce and communication. The French spoken there was rough, the manners unpolished, and the atmosphere provincial. Visitors and news from other places were rare events. (Mme Labrousse explains Bayle's lifelong mania for news and *actualités* by this early provincial isolation.)[6]

But his culture was even more isolated spiritually. If the Catholic party enjoyed the temporal advantage, the Calvinists had in recompense developed a sense of divine election, a sense of having come out of the spiritual Babylon which their contemporaries represented, and of belonging to the "little flock" to whom God in His good pleasure had promised the Kingdom. They looked upon themselves as the restorers and preservers of the pristine simplicity of God's truth, looking with special horror upon three aspects of Catholicism which they considered to be idolatry, superstition, and paganism.[7]

The paganistic element was, in their eyes, visible in the elaborate Catholic ritual, the origins of which they attributed to unauthorized and corrupting borrowings from pagan religions. Superstition they saw in the numerous miracles of the saints and the virgin which had become part of the Church's baggage during the Middle Ages. Idolatry was the "culte rendu aux créatures," that is, to the Host which during the Mass was worshipped as God by the Catholics, but which for the Protestants remained only bread. These views, representing a tradition of some one hundred fifty years standing, were a wall irrevocably dividing the minority Calvinists from the dominant Catholics. It was not possible to hold this Calvinist position and remain indifferent because these views provoked strong reaction on the part of the Catholics and had to be either defended or abandoned.

Such religious isolationism was encouraged by Bayle's family life, for he was the son of a pastor, and as Mme Labrousse points out, "Pour pieusement élevé qu'il soit, il est difficile qu'un enfant catholique respire dans sa famille une atmosphère religieuse aussi constamment présente que celle où sont plongés les enfants d'un pasteur." [8] It is not at all unlikely, she continues, that young Pierre had had only rare and superficial acquaintance with any Catholics during his early life. (Except for the eighteen months spent as a Catholic in Toulouse, he lived all of his life among Calvinists in a Calvinist environment.)

At the same time, another aspect of Protestantism made total isolationism impossible. To be a Protestant was to follow the way of individual examination, which meant that each believer had to study, pray, and formulate his own belief. It was to be obligated to follow the admonition of St. Paul to "prove all things and hold fast to that which is good," which meant studying the views of one's opponent. Moreover, the highly unpopular stance of affirming the grievous error of the Catholic majority made it necessary for the Protestants to follow another injunction of St. Paul, that is, to be ready at any moment to "give a reason for the faith that is in you." To be open and to be aware of other points of view were qualities more dominant at some times and places than at others, but both were genuinely parts of the Protestant tradition. Bayle developed them in his youth along with a certain sectarianism and provincialism to be expected from his early milieu.

Bayle's early faith was likewise conditioned by the Calvinist idea of God. The God to which Bayle's family and neighbors addressed their prayers in their houses and churches was majestic, personal, and immediate. He was providential, intervening in the affairs of men and nations. Before His throne, the mightiest of the world were as nothing, but even the humblest peasant might be the object of His infinite mercy. By the inspiration of His Spirit, the humble might be exalted and see the learning of the wise come to naught.

"Are we to believe that each individual, no matter how ignorant, can understand the word of God better than all of the councils of the Church?" The question was asked by Bishop Bossuet in debate with the minister Jean Claude in 1682.

The minister did not hesitate to answer, "Yes," if the individual who reads the Scriptures is enlightened by the Holy Spirit, and the councils who read them are not.[9]

It was in fact through the Holy Spirit that God's grace was manifest, the Holy Spirit which enlightened the intellect and shaped the will. It is perhaps in this sense of immanence that one finds the explanation of the intense inwardness of Calvinism. Stern, austere, and spare though its doctrines might be to the outsider, more than one Calvinist could exclaim with Jonathan Edwards, "I love the doctrines of the Gospel. They have been as green pastures to my soul."

And yet the Calvinism of Bayle's time was the antithesis of mysticism. The Calvinist emphasis on the individual was generally more productive of rationality than enthusiasm, not in so many words, but in the tacit presuppositions and spirit of the movement. The basic question of Protestant-Catholic differences was that of authority — did it reside in the individual or in the Church? It is true that when the Reformers opted for the individual, they added the significant stipulation that the individual reason must be enlightened by the Holy Spirit, yet their seemingly endless and voluminous works of controversy testified that they felt their intellects so enlightened. True, the Scriptures were the court of last appeal officially, but the practical effect of the principle of individual examination was to give more and more authority to reason, which, divinely aided or not, had to interpret the Scriptures.[10]

It is against this background that one must consider Bayle's conversion to Catholicism, which was the theological conclusion of the earnestness and intellectuality of his early religious orientation. In 1666, Pierre left the family milieu at Carla to undertake his studies at the Protestant Academy in Puylaurens. The fact that he was nineteen, that is, several years older than many of his fellow students, is revealing. The family was in less than modest financial circumstances, and Pierre's education had to wait on the availability of money, especially since the studies of his older brother Jacob had priority.[11]

The first year at the Academy was to some extent disillusioning, for the conduct of many of his classmates did not square with the scrupulously pious atmosphere to which he was accustomed and which he no doubt expected to find in a Calvinist school. The teaching staff was, in addition, not brilliant.

Another shock was in store for him. Being a curious and voracious reader, he came in contact with the writings of Catholic apologists and following the great Protestant principle of individual examination he read into them deeply to judge for himself of their worth. He found that they were not lacking in cogent reasoning when treating the basic point of the authority and infallibility of the Church.[12]

If indeed God has set over His Church a visible guide ("un juge parlant"), ran the Catholic arguments, and endowed him with infallibility in matters of doctrine, no Protestant shift or reasoning is of any avail to the contrary. When God speaks, who will presume to argue? There are, moreover, declarations in the Scripture which indicate that God intended to do just that. And what is more reasonable than to expect that God would grant perpetuity to His Church to keep men from being tossed to and fro on every wind of doctrine? Is it likely or even possible that God would permit the whole Church to fall into error and leave mankind without a guide? If these arguments are sound, the Protestants are all in schism and have departed from the way of salvation. Bayle had apparently never before encountered this line of reasoning set forth in all of its force, and it filled him with doubts.[13]

His doubts were so strong that in combination with the mediocrity and lack of fervor at Puylaurens, they caused him to take the road to Toulouse to see for himself and perhaps to take advantage of the superior teaching of the Jesuits. (He was then in his third year, doing his "philosophy.")

A priest who lodged at the same house where Bayle boarded, the "subtil controversiste" Bayle mentioned, pressed the advantage to such a point that the young errant concluded to the error of his Protestant ways and converted to the Catholic faith.

Bayle's conversion to Catholicism was not emotive or sentimental. As Mme Labrousse points out, it was hardly a conversion at all in the modern sense of the word, but it was nonetheless completely in keeping with his early background. She has this discerning comment:

> ... la décision de Pierre est un fruit authentique de ce libre examen loyal, de cet effort constant pour approfondir la vérité dont on vit sans se laisser arrêter par aucun respect humain, ce qui est sans doute la plus précieuse des traditions spirituelles des réformés; et d'autre part elle manifeste ce souci d'une répercussion immédiate de la théorie sur la pratique que met au premier rang le moralisme impérieux si jalousement cultivé par les protestants. Ni humble, ni dévote, ni frémissante, à la fois honnête, orgueilleuse et naïve, telle nous apparaît la démarche de l'étudiant. Ce qu'on ne saurait contester, c'est que, loin de laisser discerner en lui un penchant naissant pour le scepticisme, elle témoigne au contraire d'une belle confiance dans la raison et les raisonnements. ... (I, 73, 74)

But had he perhaps not been deceived by these same reasons and reasonings? He had not been long at Toulouse before he began to be offended by several aspects of Catholic doctrine and practice, especially "le culte excessif rendu aux créatures." Even if the Pope were God's duly established vicar, twenty-one years of Calvinist simplicity and horror of "idolatry" and "superstition" were not a felicitous preparation for processions, saints' days, miracles, and rituals.

And what about the Pope and the authority of the Church to which the individual was to bow? The demanding logic and dialectics which he was learning from the Jesuits were perhaps too effective, for they led him to conclude that there had been some sophistry in arguments to which he had succumbed.[14] He was confirmed in these sentiments by frequent conversations which he had with his cousin, Naudis de Bruguière, who now lodged with him and persisted in pointing out to Bayle that "whatever submission the church of Rome exacts, it was notwithstanding by the way of examination, that they thought fit to bring about his conversion."[15] Upon careful examination of his cousin's argument, Bayle found it valid and concluded that the very procedure by which the Jesuits had converted him refuted their own argument and established the supremacy of the Protestant principle of individual examination: the final authority in religious belief had to be the individual and not the church because the church had been obligated to establish its authority by appeal to the individual. The difficulty about the authority of the church and the objection to the way of examination were thus resolved (and this was the only argument which had brought Bayle into Catholicism), and he felt intellectually obligated to return to his original faith.

Bayle's return to the Reformed Church was not brought about solely by intellectual factors, however. It was accompanied and hastened by an element of emotion and a spiritual experience which left a lasting impression on Bayle's personality and which influenced to some degree the future direction of his thought.

A good part of this emotional experience was associated with his family, but Bayle's family ties were inevitably bound up with his religious profession: both his older brother and his father were ministers, and it was his adherence to Catholicism which separated him from his family. In this light, the circumstances of his abjuration of Catholicism are especially revealing. A friend of the Bayle family, De Pradals de Larbon, had gained young Pierre's confidence. The two often dined together at Toulouse, and one day Bayle confided his misgivings to his friend, having, as his friend Des Maizeaux puts it, found several doctrines in the Romish religion, which appeared to him contrary both to reason and scripture. Mr. de Pradals, charmed with this confession, presently communicated it to Mr. Bayle's family, to their inexpressible satisfaction. They presently resolved to send his older brother to him, and begged of Mr. de Pradals to manage the interview. Mr. Bayle's elder brother having gone to Toulouse with Mr. de Pradals, the latter invited young Bayle to dine with him, as it was his custom to do. After some discourse, when the servants had retired, Mr. Bayle the elder, who was in a closet, came out and shewed himself to his brother. All that joy, grief, and surprize have most strong at once seized the young Bayle, so that he was not able to utter a word, he threw himself at his feet, and burst out into tears. Mr. Bayle, the elder, could not refrain his, and raising him up he spoke to him in so tender a manner, that the young Bayle discovered the bottom of his heart to him, by telling him how impatient he was to leave Toulouse, and renounce the errors which had seduced him.[16]

Several days after, Bayle secretly left Toulouse and formally abjured Catholicism in the presence of his brother and three other ministers of the area. It was the solicitude of his brother together with the mutual shedding of tears which caused Bayle to confess his anxiety (which he had evidently felt for some time) and errors and to reveal his desire to leave Toulouse. All of the elements which usually accompany conversion and formation of conviction are present — anxiety, confession, forgiveness, and strong expression of emotion.

It is possible that Des Maizeaux's account is to some extent romanticized, but a letter which Bayle wrote three months later shows that he regarded his brother as a divine instrument in bringing about his return to Protestantism and that he felt his deliverance from Catholicism, which he had come to regard as a spiritual bondage or darkness, to be due to nothing less than the power *(vertu)* of God. Upon his arrival at Geneva after abjuring Catholicism, he wrote to his brother as follows:

> Nous ne sommes plus dans le temps du mystère, nous sommes dans le temps de la manifestation, si bien que ne goûtant pas le bien que nous attendions en espérance seulement, mais en ayant la pleine et entière jouissance, il ne reste plus que de se réjouir au Seigneur qui a fait cette grand'oeuvre, et de lui en rendre grâces immortelles. Pour moi j'ai regardé ma sortie hors de cette ville superstitieuse où j'ai fait quelque séjour [Toulouse] avec la même joie qu'ont ceux qui habitent sous les pôles de revoir le soleil après une absence de six mois, et j'ai remercié Dieu de ce grand bienfait comme d'une délivrance et d'une rédemption très ardemment attendue. Je ne doute pas que vous n'en ayez fait encore plus, vous dont les prières ont comme hâté le temps où Dieu voulait déployer sa vertu et qui par vos soupirs et par vos gémissements avez comme forcé le Tout Puissant à me ressusciter, et le Souverain Pasteur des âmes à me ramener au petit troupeau.[17]

The tone of this letter would tend to bear out the affirmation of Victor Delbos, who maintained that Bayle's reconversion gave him an impression of the reality of grace, which is different from and beyond the scope of reason: "Ce n'était point là pure instabilité mentale; il ne pouvait vivre quelque temps avec certaines traditions [catholiques] sans en sentir avant tout l'insuffisance intellectuelle. Mais de plus, s'il reste protestant, il avait comme réservé en lui un sentiment profound de ce qui, dans les oeuvres de la nature comme dans celles de la grâce, ne se laisse jamais réduire à des raisons claires."[18] This impression was certainly more than temporary, for eleven years later (in 1681, at the time he was writing the *Pensées diverses sur la comète,* the supposed "manifesto of reason") he expressed the belief that there were "deep works of grace" which were beyond the scope of philosophy or rational explanation. Writing to his older brother, he indicated that he saw several inadequacies not only in Cartesianism but also in all other systems and added: "Il n'y en a point encore qui ait frappé au but, jamais on n'y frappera apparemment, tant sont grandes les profondeurs de Dieu dans les oeuvres de la nature, aussi bien que dans celles de la grâce."[19]

Bayle had indeed miscalculated either in leaving the Reform or in coming back to it. Both decisions were, nonetheless, sincerely made, and both of them were approved and dictated by reason and reasonings. It seems more likely to conclude that Bayle's faith in himself and the powers of his intellect were shaken more than his faith in God. As Mme Labrousse remarks, ". . . le choc décisif reçu à Toulouse, c'est d'avoir découvert combien la réalité concrète est plus complexe que les vues que l'esprit peut en prendre et d'avoir commencé à soupçonner que la compréhension des choses requiert qu'on scrute attentivement 'l'histoire . . . , l'événement . . . , l'expérience.'"[20]

As for the authenticity of his reconversion, there can be no doubt. A thought can best be judged by the act which it produces, and the fact of accepting exile for his belief testifies that he was indeed sincere.

Bayle's faith, rooted in the traditions of the Reform, was thus more probably strengthened than weakened by his two conversions. Professor Barber suggested, "It seems more probable that the real victim of the conflict was not so much his ability to hold sincere religious convictions as [ultimately] his confidence in the validity of rational argument where matters of faith are concerned."[21] Accordingly, he was later able to make the persuasion of conscience the basis of belief and to speak of the efficacy of grace in all intellectual honesty, without the ironic tone of Voltaire. And he was thus able to remain in the Reformed Church even when he concluded that its doctrines were not completely defensible on rational grounds.

NOTES

1. Mme Labrousse has two very thorough and perspicacious chapters on the conversion and reconversion of Bayle in *Pierre Bayle*, I, 50–93. Her work in this, as in other areas, has largely replaced Des Maizeaux's "Vie de Bayle," which appears in the Preface of the *Dictionnaire* after 1730.

2. This is a point that Rex makes in "Pierre Bayle, Louis Tronchin et la querelle des donatistes: Etude d'un document inédit du XVIIe siècle," *BSHPF*, CV (July–Sept., 1959), 104–105.

3. Lenient, *Etude*, p. 27.

4. Deschamps, *Genèse*, p. 126.

5. Delvolvé, *Essai*, p. 11.

6. Labrousse, *Pierre Bayle*, I, 32–33.

7. *Ibid.*, p. 50–51.

8. *Ibid.*, p. 52.

9. Cited by Paul Hazard, *La Crise*, p. 72, note.

10. Prof. Rex has devoted one thorough chapter to tracing the development of a strong current of rationalism within the Reformed Church, in *Essays*, pp. 80–120.

11. Labrousse, *Pierre Bayle*, I, 25–27.

12. *Ibid.*, pp. 62–71.

13. *Ibid.*, pp. 68–69. Prof. Rex also describes this aspect of Protestant-Catholic controversies in *Essays*, pp. 5–8.

14. See Bayle's own retrospective account in *CCR, OD*, II, 739.

15. The wording is Des Maizeaux's in his "Life of Bayle," vii. The English translation is cited here.

16. *Ibid.*

17. Letter to Jacob Bayle, 2 Nov 70, ed. J. L. Gerig and G. L. van Roosbroeck in "Unpublished Letters of Pierre Bayle," *The Romanic Review*, XXIII (1932), 216–217. The fact that this aspect of Bayle's conversion has been overlooked is explained by the truncated form in which the letter appeared in the eighteenth-century editions of Bayle's correspondence; the reference to Bayle's exalted fervor had been omitted, and in several places the text had been emended.

18. Delbos, *La Philosophie française* (Paris, 1919), p. 147.

19. 29 May 81, *LFam, OD*, I, 126. The *Lettres de M. Bayle à sa famille* in the first volume of his *Oeuvres diverses* are paginated separately.

20. Labrousse, *Pierre Bayle*, I, 92.

21. Barber, "Faith and Reason," p. 112.

4   The Roots of Reason

IF Bayle's arrival in Geneva marked his spiritual return to the Reformed Church, it also marked his return to it intellectually and signaled the beginning of a new phase of his intellectual life. The leaven of Cartesianism was spreading throughout Europe and had entered into the Reform through the liberal, though orthodox, Calvinists of the Protestant Academy of Saumur. Two of Bayle's professors at Geneva were Salmurians, Robert Chouet and Louis Tronchin, and for the next six years he was to be under their rationalistic influence.[1]

There is no suggestion during Bayle's four-year stay in Switzerland that he felt any conflict between Cartesian rationalism and the orthodox faith. The Salmurians felt just as strongly as did Malebranche later on that there could be no conflict between the natural and heavenly light. Each complemented the other, of which Bayle soon had a convincing example in his courses with Tronchin.

The young postulant had just been reconverted, in part, by unanswerable objections to the Catholic doctrine of Transubstantiation and the infallibility of the Church. Now Tronchin reaffirmed his convictions by drawing other edifying and cogent arguments from the Cartesian philosophy. "Au reste," Bayle wrote to his father, "vous ne sauriez croire quels avantages il tire de la philosophie de M. Descartes dont il fait assez ouverte profession, pour combattre ceux de l'Eglise romaine."[2]

But it was this same rationalism that served the defense of the faith so well at Geneva which was to clash sharply with revelation in his mature years. The reason for the clash was in large measure due to the critical mode of thought and method of disputation which characterized his writings throughout the rest of his life.

He had already gotten a good start at Toulouse where he had

learned the power of the scholastic logic and dialectic. "C'était un temps où je disputais assez bien," he wrote later, "je venais frais émoulu d'une école où on m'avait bien enseigné la chicanerie scolastique, et je puis dire sans vanité que je ne m'en acquittais pas trop mal."[3] It was a formidable and highly-prized weapon for a Protestant who was often on the defensive, an essential part of one's baggage in a milieu where disputation played such a large role. Accordingly, he counseled his younger brother Joseph: "Accoutumez-vous de bonne heure à faire jouer l'imagination et à l'exercer sur les concepts et les formalités. Cela sera d'usage dans la suite et vous accoutumera à la méthode et à la justesse. Il n'est rien de plus redoutable qu'un habile homme qui est bon logicien, il vous renverse les livres les plus solides, et à moins d'être bon logicien, il est impossible de lui tenir tête."[4] Eighteen years later he felt that the advice was still good and counseled his cousin's sons to develop the scholastic method "de pousser vivement et subtilement une objection et de répondre nettement et précisément aux difficultés."[5]

To the "chicanerie scolastique" Bayle added the Cartesian method he found so admirably exemplified in the lectures of Tronchin. Bayle's enthusiasm for a new discovery is unmistakable:

> Il est dégagé de toutes les opinions populaires et de ces sentiments généraux qui ont été crus par ceux qui nous ont précédés, sans être soutenus de l'autorité de l'Ecriture. Ce n'est rien pour lui d'alléguer qu'un tel et un tel, les universités, les académies ont condamné une chose; il examine les raisons de leur conduite. S'il les trouve justes, il les embrasse, et non autrement. Ses leçons sont des chefs-d'oeuvre et une critique fine et délicate du commun des théologiens . . . il remarque les fausses preuves . . . les passages de l'Ecriture mal appliqués . . . les mauvaises réponses aux arguments des adversaires . . .[6]

Bayle adopted the rigor of this method and recommended it also to his younger brother: "La maxime de Descartes est la plus raisonnable du monde, que pour éviter de se tromper il n'est rien tel que de suspendre son jugement jusqu'à ce qu'on ait examiné les choses avec la dernière exactitude, et qu'il n'y a point de source d'erreurs plus féconde que la précipitation de juger."[7]

This early training, together with Bayle's naturally incisive intellect and fairmindedness, produced a dialectic which was exacting and exhaustive. One of its basic principles was that one should advance nothing which could be objected to rationally or empirically, or which could be retorted against one's own argument. His writings and correspondence abound with comments which show that he therefore refused to support any affirmation by faulty reasoning or unsound evidence, believing, for example, that certain moralists had destroyed confidence in moral principles because they ". . . se servent souvent des raisonnements faux et les font valoir comme démonstrations incontestables."[8] In a letter to his brother, he likewise condemned a Protestant author (Jurieu) who had made use of falsified information in a new book entitled *L'Esprit de M. Arnaud.*[9] In his journal he praised an Anabaptist author for attacking the credibility of pagan oracles, even though they had been used to defend Christianity, maintaining that "il serait indigne du nom chrétien d'appuyer la plus sainte et la plus auguste de toutes les vérités sur une tradition erronée . . . il serait aussi d'une dangereuse conséquence, surtout dans un siècle philosophique comme celui où nous vivons."[10] And in the *Dictionnaire* he reflected that in writing for people who think and weigh each argument it is better not to answer than to answer badly because ". . . d'autres ont remarqué que rien n'est plus pernicieux que d'employer de mauvais raisonnements contre les impies."[11]

When was an opponent bested? Bayle was not satisfied until he had refuted the strongest arguments of his adversary on his opponent's own ground, and it was therefore characteristic of him to shun the commonplaces of disputes and assume some common ground upon which his opponent could be bested with his own principles or arguments. In the preface to the *Pensées diverses,* he stated that because the Sorbonne doctor to whom the work was addressed would object to a philosophical treatment of the subject, he (Bayle) would agree to use only theological arguments, "car je ne veux pas que vous m'échappiez."[12] On the other hand, for those who wanted to make experience the only standard, he would argue from experience in order to "battre les gens jusques sur leur propre fumier."[13] It was this principle which determined his approach to the question of tolerance in the *Commentaire philosophique.* Realizing that without a common ground the controversialists could live as long as Methuselah and still not end the dispute, Bayle reduced the question to the terms of ethics, which both sides accepted.[14]

In addition to being exacting, Bayle's dialectic was also exhaustive, for it required the disputant to foresee, state and answer every possible objection to his thesis, and this often made Bayle's writings extremely prolix and complex. For example, in the *Pensées diverses* the first sixty-nine pages are devoted to the presentation of the thesis and the next hundred to answering possible objections. The famous examples of virtuous atheists are invoked to prove the seventh proof of the seventh proof of the fourth answer to the first objection to the proposition that comets are not the sign of misfortune! In the *Supplément du Commentaire philosophique* where he sets out to ruin the "dernière échappatoire" of his adversaries, he presents and refutes possible objections during the course of twenty pages *in-folio,* after which he says, "Il est bien temps de revenir au point capital de cette dispute, après avoir suivi nos adversaires dans tous les faux-fuyants et tous les retranchements qu'ils pourraient opposer à notre poursuite."[15]

It was Bayle's intention in so doing to make his conclusions as clear and evident as possible, for he excused his prolixity by saying that "on ne convainc jamais son lecteur par les raisons qu'on lui apporte, si on n'a soin de prévoir les difficultés qu'il se pourra faire lui-même."[16] Ironically, his exhaustiveness is the very thing that has made him misunderstood — in endeavoring to follow Bayle through the complexities of his argument, the reader is quite likely to lose sight of the original intent. Is Bayle stating his own position or is he only stating the strongest arguments of the opposition in order to refute them more completely? Is he stating a universal principle or is he merely answering the objection to the answer to the objection? He wrote for those who thought in syllogisms as he did, and who were inured to the exhaustive sifting and winnowing of arguments which this method of disputation entailed, but it was inevitable that he would be misunderstood by the public in general who did not take the trouble to follow his arguments through many *in-folio* pages.[17]

This hybrid combination of scholastic logic and disputation, the critical method of Descartes, and the Protestant principle of individual examination also wielded an enormous influence on the development of Bayle's thought. To be Protestant was not only to be obliged to "examine all things." It was also to be constantly caught in the tension of intellectual challenge. Now one may believe on subjective grounds, but if one presumes to answer an opponent one must follow the way of logic, which is to abstract oneself from questions of party interest, to be a spectator before one is a participant, and to form conclusions only according to the soundness of the evidence.[18] One effect of this rigor and fairmindedness was to prepare Bayle for his future role as editor of *Les Nouvelles de la République des Lettres.*

More important is the fact that Bayle came to think of reason as primarily a critical tool. Emphasizing analysis rather than synthesis, it trained his mind to act more as a crucible for testing some proposition already formulated than as a forge for creating some new system. Moreover, it was principally this early training that led him to conclude that a proposition was rationally certain only when every possible objection to it had been answered and when it had been established by principles as evident as Descartes' *cogito.* He explained this in the *Commentaire philosophique* (1686), where he commented that

> le critère de la vérité . . . est une idée si claire et si distincte que nous sentions vivement que la chose ne peut être que comme cela, après avoir bien considéré toutes les raisons de douter, je veux dire toutes les instances des adversaires. . . . On appelle *criterium veritatis* . . . l'évidence irrésistible avec laquelle nous connaissons que le tout est plus grand que sa partie, que si de choses égales on ôte choses égales les résidus seront égaux, que six est la moitié de douze, etc.[19]

Therefore, when the exigencies of the Protestant-Catholic controversy (*ca.* 1685) led him first to ferret out all of the weak points of both sides and to conclude that reason could find possible objections to *any* theology or philosophic system, reason was more fit to destroy than to build up, and this was a major step toward the fideism to be expressed in the *Dictionnaire*.

But while Bayle was developing a critical method which was to prove so inimical to theology, he was being imbued with another view of reason which was to have the opposite effect. For him the strong ethical orientation of Calvinism yielded the principle that the mark of the true Church and the chief concern of religion were virtue, not speculation, morality and not theology. And especially in the Salmurian tradition which so influenced Bayle at Geneva, the natural light of reason and the supernatural light of revelation were never at variance in questions of ethics, whatever might be the deficiencies of reason in other areas.[20]

The severely moral and even Puritanical orientation of his childhood and adolescence had, in fact, made him aware of the moral shortcomings of some of his own party. In 1671, for example, Geneva was divided by a dispute over universal and individual grace. The civil authorities had been obliged to impose silence on both parties in order to keep the peace. With his customary fairness, Bayle studied out the arguments of both sides, and wrote to his father that ". . . selon mon petit jugement . . . la question en elle-même est de très petite conséquence pour le salut [et] on peut être indifféremment de l'opinion qu'on voudra sans qu'il y ait rien à perdre ou à gagner. . . ." Bayle found that neither side had understood the other and that this question had only been the occasion for jealousy, bad feeling, and revenge among the disputants. He then added significantly: "Quoi qu'il en soit, j'ai eu le plaisir de voir, si toutefois il n'y a pas plus sujet de pleurer que de se divertir en voyant les faiblesses de l'homme, que pour être professeur en théologie, on n'est pas moins le jouet des passions, de la colère, de l'envie, et de la vengeance."[21]

When he saw the purity of the Reform being compromised by the laxity of certain of the Protestant ministry, he insisted repeatedly that the Church could not retain divine approval if it were morally corrupt. In a letter to his younger brother Joseph, who was then studying for the ministry, he lamented the lack of virtue among postulants in the Protestant academies, stating that if God did not confer the leadership of the Reformed Church on those of good faith and morals, He would not have any more relation with it than with the various pagan societies.[22]

In another letter to Joseph six months later, he developed the same theme and indicated that he considered moral deviation more serious than theological deviation:

> Ce que vous dites de la diminution des philosophes et de la corruption qui règne dans l'Académie m'afflige mortellement, surtout le dernier article, parce que c'est une chose qui couvre de honte et diffame notre réformation et nous fait regarder comme des schismatiques qui n'ont eu pour but que de se libérer du pesant joug de l'abstinence et de la mortification de la chair, ce qui rend les gens plus odieux que s'ils faisaient bande à part pour ne pouvoir croire certaines doctrines de spéculation, comme ont fait les Arminiens en Hollande. La mollesse de nos directeurs en cela . . . me paraît encore plus déplorable que le libertinage de la jeunesse. . . .[23]

This belief in the pre-eminence of morality and in the futility and harm of theological dispute, together with this awareness of the moral laxness of a part of his own party, was to have a profound effect on Bayle's future thought. It helped him to formulate the doctrine of the "erring conscience" without believing himself in the least unorthodox, and it permitted him in good faith to reduce the terms of the Protestant-Catholic dispute to the broadest principles of morality. Later, in his dispute with Jurieu, he was able to apply these same principles to elements of Protestantism without having any intention of attacking religion as a whole. Finally, it formed an integral part of his eventual fideism: morality being basic, and belief in the speculative being relatively unimportant, subjection of reason to faith in speculative matters was possible, if not painless.

A discussion of Bayle's early intellectual development would not be complete without pointing out the significance of his insatiable and universal curiosity which was in evidence from his early childhood, for it was this love of erudition which provided him throughout his life with an effective counterbalance to his propensity for reasoning.

He had always been a voracious reader and the intellectual awakening he experienced at Geneva opened new vistas. His reading was abundant but unmethodical. "Il est certain," he wrote to his older brother, "que jamais amant volage n'a pas plus souvent changé de maîtresses que moi de livres."[24]

Indications of this curiosity and penchant for erudition are evident on almost every page of Bayle's letters, especially those written in 1674 and 1675 when he was a tutor in a private family and felt cut off from the Republic of Letters. The vast amount of reading which he did also attests to this curiosity. Miss Cowdrick states that "one of the characteristics of Bayle's correspondence that most impresses the reader is the wide variety of book titles which it contains."[25] In addition, he was always eager to know current news — his favorite kind of letter was a sort of journal written over a period of weeks and which contained the happenings of each day.[26] And since his correspondence was his most fertile source of news, he considered postage his most pleasurable expense.[27] One detail alone should be sufficient to prove Bayle's inclination for pure erudition: when he wrote to his older brother about a terrible scandal concerning a noble who had slain his wife and her paramour, he was interested principally in the genealogy of the family concerned.

The importance of this curiosity to Bayle's thought was twofold. First, it further fitted him for his journalistic career as editor of the *Nouvelles de la République des Lettres* and provided him with an occupation when he tired of controversy.[28]

Secondly, it determined Bayle to follow the life of a scholar, rather than that of a minister. Two years after his arrival in Geneva he had given up his original intent of going into the ministry. Practical considerations dictated his decision, since his voice had been adversely affected by the air at Geneva. Certain friends had also dissuaded him, and there were moreover already more ministers than there were positions.[29] But it is more probable than he simply felt more inclined to a life of study rather than of preaching. His decision to give up the ministry was based largely on his temperament, at least if the following observation on the difference between scholars and preachers, which he made in 1684, can be applied to him personally:

> Un homme qui a beaucoup d'esprit et de jugement se peut servir avec avantage de la science par rapport aux prédications, mais pour l'ordinaire la profonde science nuit plus à un prédicateur qu'elle ne lui sert. D'ailleurs, comme il est rare que ceux qui sont nés pour les profondes études s'attachent aux brillants de l'éloquence, qui exigent un fort grand travail; il est rare aussi que ceux qui sont propres à la chaire aiment les profondeurs de l'érudition, qui demandent un esprit abstrait et qui se puisse accommoder de la sécheresse.[30]

Bayle left Switzerland for Rouen May 29, 1674. He had spent

two years as a tutor for a private family at Coppet near Geneva, and now wondered if he could not better his lot elsewhere. He was not the same when he left as when he arrived. He had lost much of his provincialism. He had begun to amass an impressive amount of erudition and had developed a keen and powerful dialectic. In his thought there was a leaven of rationalism at work.

What was the state of his faith?

In the article "Spinoza" of the *Dictionnaire,* written as he was nearing fifty, he spoke of those who had "religion in the mind but not in the heart." Was he among them? In the *Dictionnaire* there is indeed a singular lack of fervor in his appeal to Revelation as the sure guide out of skeptical perplexity.[31] In his letters of the same period there is resignation but little emotion or expectant confidence.

It was not so in his early years. When he left Switzerland, his worldly prospects were less than brilliant — he saw no immediate possibility of a position higher than that of a semi-domestic, he could not return to his home region, there was no future for him in Geneva, and he could re-enter France only under a pseudonym. He nonetheless wrote to his brother Jacob that

> La providence de Dieu s'étendant à tout, il faut espérer que nous y aurons quelque part, et pour moi, j'en fais toujours non mon pis aller, comme font plusieurs, mais ma principale ressource. . . . [car j'ai] dans ma maison la cause de ma confiance, me persuadant que la piéte et les saintes prières d'un père, d'une mere et d'un frère justes et craig-nants Dieu tiendront toujours le ciel ouvert en ma faveur. . . .[32]

Such expressions of faith and strong family emotion are often found in Bayle's early letters. But his mother died in 1674, his father and younger brother in 1684, and his older brother Jacob (the pastor) died in 1685 as a result of the anti-Protestant persecutions, and after this period the religious tone of his letters changes from confidence to resignation in face of the increasing irrationality of God's world.

But as he left Switzerland, his confidence was high. He spent about eighteen months as a tutor for a family in Rouen, after which he found a position as professor of history and philosophy at the Protestant Academy of Sedan, where he remained for over five years. Then in 1681 the Academy was closed by order of Louis XIV, and Pierre Bayle went into exile a second time.

NOTES

1. See Rex, *Essays*, pp. 128–132.
2. Unedited letter from the Bibliothèque nationale, fonds français, ms. 12771, cited by Rex, *Essays*, pp. 135–136.
3. Letter to Basnage, 5 May 75, *OD*, IV, 597.
4. 6 May 77, *LFam*, *OD*, I, 77. See also the letter from Pierre to Joseph dated March 28, 1677, in *LFam*, *OD*, I, 74.
5. Letter to his cousin, 27 Jan 95, *LFam*, *OD*, I, 174. Bayle had two cousins — de Naudis and De Bruguières — with whom he corresponded. In subsequent references, when there is no indication as to which one was the intended recipient of the letter, the note will state simply "to his cousin."
6. Letter to his father, 21 Sept 71, *LFam*, *OD*, I, 10.
7. 3 Nov 78, *NL*, II, 7–8.
8. Letter to Minutoli, 13 Oct 74, in *Choix de la correspondance inédite de Pierre Bayle*, ed. Emile Gigas (Copenhagen, 1890), p. 43.
9. 9 Jan 84, *NL*, II, 213.
10. *NRL*, March 1684, *OD*, I, 4.
11. *DHC*, "Socin," note 0, III, 2615.
12. *PDC*, *OD*, III, 12.
13. *PDC*, *OD*, III, 4.
14. *CP*, *OD*, II, 391.
15. *SCP*, *OD*, II, 517.
16. *SCP*, *OD*, II, 517. See also *SCP*, p. 478.
17. Dibon, *Pierre Bayle, le philosophe de Rotterdam*, p. xiii.
18. See, for example, the letter from Bayle to his older brother, 21 January 79, *NL*, where Bayle, though unmistakably Protestant at this time, gives credit to the logic of certain Jansenist authors who were writing against the Protestants and adjudges them the victors when their arguments are the stronger.
19. *CP*, *OD*, II, 438.
20. Rex, *Essays*, pp. 91, 95–97.
21. 21 Sept 71, *LFam*, *OD*, I, 9–10.
22. 28 March 77, *LFam*, *OD*, I, 75.
23. 16 Nov 77, *LFam*, *OD*, I, 82–83. According to Frank Puaux, some of the most eminent Protestant leaders of the time were voicing the same opinion. Claude, the foremost Protestant minister and champion of the Reform against Bousset, frequently preached on this subject. See Puaux, *Les Précurseurs français de la tolérance au XVIIe siècle* (Paris, 1880), p. 94.
24. 21 Sept 71, *LFam*, *OD*, I, 13.
25. Cowdrick, *Early Reading*, p. 42.
26. Letter to his older brother, 17 Dec 78, *NL*, II, 28–29.
27. Letter to his younger brother, 3 Nov 78, *NL, II,* 14.
28. 26 Dec 78, *NL*, II, 62–63.
29. Letter to his older brother, 2 July 72, *LFam*, *OD*, I, 20.
30. *NLC*, *OD*, II, 297-298.
31. Prof. Richard Popkin discusses this remark of Bayle in "The High Road to Pyrrhonism," *American Philosophical Quarterly*, II (January, 1965), pp. 12–13.
32. Cited by Labrousse, *Pierre Bayle*, I, 121–122.

5 Reason, Morals, and Superstition

WHEN Bayle arrived in Rotterdam in the fall of 1681 as a part of the general exodus of Huguenot refugees, he had with him only a few personal effects and the prospect of a rather ill-paying position at the *École illustre* of Rotterdam.

But if the royal edicts had wiped out his prospects and position in France, they had also given him a clean slate and put him on an equal footing with his fellow refugees. No longer classed according to his beginnings or his poverty, he was freer to develop by his own merits than had he remained in France.[1]

He was likewise beginning to mature intellectually. In his trunk was a bulky manuscript on comets, omens, superstitions, politics, morals, atheism, and other "miscellaneous" thoughts. It appeared in print in March of 1682 bearing the title *Lettre à M.L.A.D.C., docteur de Sorbonne: Où il est prouvé par plusieurs raisons tirées de la philosophie et de la théologie que les comètes ne sont point le présage d'aucun malheur. Avec plusieurs réflexions morales et politiques et plusieurs observations historiques et la réfutation de quelques erreurs populaires.*

Long, prolix, digressive, it has been one of the most difficult to interpret of Bayle's works. The traditional view has been that this work was both an apology for the authority of reason and an attack upon belief in the supernatural, the critics having either equated superstition with the supernatural or else having taken Catholicism to be the sum total of Christianity. Delvolvé, for instance, saw in the piece an effort to undermine religious belief generally by separating belief from morality. The superstitions which Bayle attacked, according to Delvolvé, "offraient des conditions particulièrement favorables à une étude du préjugé: assez distinctes des dogmes chrétiens pour que la critique ne fût pas dangereuse; assez proches de ces dogmes

35

pour qu'elle portât généralement sur les croyances surnaturelles." And in another connection he commented: "En réalité, ce n'est pas entre l'athéisme et l'idolâtrie que la question de la valeur morale s'agite: c'est entre l'athéisme et tout dogme surnaturel."[2]

Paul Hazard was of a similar opinion, feeling that Bayle found an element of idolatory in all religions (and most certainly in the religion of his day). Thus, in reasoning that not even atheism was a greater evil than idolatry, said Hazard, and in pointing out the vices of Christians and the virtues of atheists, Bayle had in reality used his dissertation on comets to glorify atheism.[3]

But nowhere in Bayle's writings is it more important to keep sight of the context of his remarks. Due to the prolixity of his method and the discursiveness of his intellect, the possibilities of ambiguity are legion.

What are the arguments set forth in the *Pensées diverses?*

The only authorities invoked in favor of comets, Bayle begins, are untrustworthy: poets and historians lie by profession, and tradition only relays what they have set forth. Moreover, comets cannot be divine signs because (1) comets do not have the power of causing any physical effect on the earth; (2) if they did, it could just as easily result in good fortune as bad fortune; (3) astrology, which has been the foundation of the predictions concerning comets, is only a pagan superstition; (4) even if woes and misfortunes had followed comets, the comets would have been neither the sign nor the cause thereof; (5) the number of misfortunes has been no greater after the appearance of comets than before; (6) universal consent is of no value in proving that comets cause or foreshadow misfortunes because many errors were once universally received; (7) if comets were omens of misfortune, God would have performed miracles in order to confirm idolatry; (8) the belief that comets are harbingers of public catastrophe is a pagan superstition which was introduced into and fostered in Christianity by an undue reverence for antiquity.

In true scholastic fashion, Bayle then undertakes to forestall any possible objections that his doctor might have. The first objection was that God formed comets in order that the pagans might recognize the workings of Providence and thus keep from falling into atheism. Bayle answers that this is impossible because (1) God does not eradicate one crime only to establish another in its stead; (2) the pagans, far from falling into atheism, were continually multiplying the number of their gods, independently of any divine sign; (3) even if it were to be feared that atheism would replace idolatry, miracles would not have been necessary to prevent atheism, the effects of nature, the political motives of rulers, and the self-interest of the priests being sufficient to do this; (4) atheism is not a worse evil than idolatry. This last point is established by seven proofs: (1) imperfection is at least as contrary to the nature of God as non-existence; (2) the Church Fathers held that idolatry was the greatest of all crimes; (3) idolators were atheists in a certain sense; (4) the knowledge of God only makes the crimes of an idolator worse; (5) idolatry makes people more difficult to convert than does atheism; (6) neither the mind nor the heart of an idolator is superior to that of an atheist; (7) atheism does not necessarily corrupt morals, because man does not act according to his profession but according to his passions.

Bayle then supports this last idea by showing that there are numerous people who have believed in God and yet committed the most terrible crimes, examples being the Crusaders, soldiers in Christian armies, prostitutes, the devils in Hell, everyday people, many criminals who were devoted to the Holy Virgin, and those Christians who frequently go to Mass and who yet correct their conduct only from purely human motives. In this, remarks Bayle, the Christians are no different than a society of atheists would be, all acting from the same universal human motives. This digression on atheism accounts for fifty pages *in-folio,* or about one-third of the book, after which Bayle comes back to the objection which he has been answering so deviously (that God sends comets to keep idolators from falling into atheism) and gives a fifth answer to it by pointing out that there is no example of God ever having done miracles to convert anyone to idolatry.

He then foresees a second objection: comets are formed without any miracles, but God nonetheless uses them and can perform other miracles to make Himself known among the infidels and to render them inexcusable for their idolatry. This Bayle answers by arguing (1) that unless comets were formed miraculously, they could not possibly be signs; (2) that God does no miracle among the pagans except to confirm the preaching of His Word; (3) that God did not intend to convert pagan nations by means of comets because people are not any more apt to know God after seeing a comet than they were before; and (4) that comets are not capable of leading people to a knowledge of the true God. Bayle then poses a third possible objection, that is, that comets are indeed the cause of the misfortunes which follow them. He then answers with a discussion of Malebranche's philosophy, and this is followed by observations on the contemporary European political scene to show that one could conclude nothing certain from the apparition of a comet.

Within the framework of the *Pensées diverses,* many statements appear concerning the authority of reason, which, taken alone, would tend to confirm the traditional interpretations of a Voltairian Bayle. In the preface to his "letter," for example, Bayle rebukes the doctor, who is a Sorbonne graduate in theology and who believes that comets are indeed portents of misfortunes and divine judgments. Why has he accepted this error and neglected to consult the oracle of reason? Bayle then answers his own question:

> C'est que vous croyez qu'il y a quelque chose de divin dans tout ceci ... c'est que vous imaginez que le consentement général de tant de nations ... ne peut venir que d'une espèce d'inspiration, *vox populi, vox Dei;* c'est que vous êtes accoutumé par votre caractère de théologien à ne plus raisonner dès que vous croyez qu'il y a du mystère; ce qui est une docilité fort louable, mais qui ne laisse pas d'empiéter sur les droits de la raison, comme l'a fort bien remarqué M. Pascal. ... Tout cela, monsieur, fait un sophisme d'autorité à votre esprit dont vous ne sauriez vous défendre avec toute l'adresse qui vous fait si bien démêler les faux raisonnements des logiciens.[4]

Elsewhere Bayle affirms that it is only reason which rescues one from superstition, giving as an example the popular belief in astrology which has been uprooted only by the advent of a sound and critical philosophy (p. 22). He later elaborates on the same idea: anything which resembles superstition must be tried in the crucible of reason, even though superstition has been used to support the truths of religion; for otherwise one would have to approve the conduct of those who perpetuate pious frauds, teach fables, and invent miracles whenever they believe that they will be able to increase devotion by so doing (p. 60). In this same connection he maintains that reason thus exercised cannot but lead one into a more genuine worship of God, by saying that "[nous devons donc] être bien aise que les philosophes chrétiens nous délivrent de tous les préjugés qui seraient capables de souiller la beauté mâle et solide de notre dévotion" (p. 61).

He does not except even the most universal and ancient errors and points out in particular the weakness of the popular argument by universal consent: "Un sentiment ne peut devenir probable par la multitude de ceux qui la suivent qu'autant qu'il a paru vrai à plusieurs, indépendamment de toute prévention et par la seule force d'un examen judicieux, accompagné d'exactitude et d'une grande intelligence des choses ... un témoin qui a vu est plus croyable que dix qui parlent par oui-dire" (p. 35).

But if Voltaire and the Encyclopedists were to repeat and embroider these and similar remarks of Bayle, Bayle himself was simply repeating and embroidering the arguments of the orthodox

Calvinist rationalism of his predecessors and contemporaries. Here the recent study of Walter Rex on the issues and tactics of religious controversy[5] which are always in the background of all of Bayle's writings is especially important and revealing. Protestant polemicists had not limited their appeal to the authority of the Scripture. They had called upon the testimony of reason and the senses and invoked these three criteria according to their needs. As mentioned previously (Chapter III), superstition had always been one of the main targets of the Calvinists, and Bayle was not deviating at all from the religious context of the Reform in invoking reason to destroy superstition and the grounds for believing in it.

It is also significant in this same connection that Bayle assigns supremacy to critical reason only in areas where there is no revelation. Far from trying to associate superstition with all belief in the supernatural, Bayle specifically distinguishes between the two, upbraiding, for example, those who defend their belief in superstition by scriptural analogies (*PDC,* p. 69). Moreover, in showing that eclipses and comets are neither the sign nor cause of misfortunes, Bayle does not deny the possibility of true signs sent from God. He merely indicates that in order for them to be signs to a rational being, "... il faudrait que Dieu les eût données pour signes; ou en nous faisant connaître que ces maux dépendent des éclipses comme de leur cause naturelle; ou en nous disant qu'il veut que nous soyons avertis de nos malheurs par le moyen des éclipses. Dieu n'a fait ni l'un ni l'autre; par conséquent, les éclipses ne sont point des signes." In order for something to be a sign to a rational being it must neither depend on the course of nature nor announce something which happens every year anyway (pp. 38–39). To bear this out, Bayle points out that when God did give a sign at the time of the Crucifixion, He chose a time of day when the darkness could not be natural (p. 44).

Later on, he foresees the possible objection that it is audacious for him to deny God has done some miraculous thing on the grounds that his "petite raison" does not understand it. He then makes his position more explicit, saying:

> Sur cela, monsieur, je vous déclare que ... c'est assez pour moi de savoir que Dieu a fait une chose pour ne douter point qu'il ne l'ait faite avec une souveraine raison. ... De sorte que si l'on me pouvait prouver ou par des raisons nécessaires, ou par une autorité infaillible, que Dieu forme les comètes miraculeusement pour nous être signe de sa colére, j'y acquiescerais de tout mon coeur, quoi que je crusse voir par mes lumières qu'il n'y a rien de plus inutile aux intérêts du vrai Dieu, ni même de plus favorable aux intérêts du Démon que des miracles de cette nature. Mais nous ne sommes pas en ces termes (p. 137).

Because there is no revelation on the subject, one must proceed by reason and experience to see what is more compatible with God's holiness and attributes, but this, insists Bayle, is far from subjecting the Scripture to the same examination (p. 138). It was entirely characteristic of Bayle at this time to oppose any Biblical exegesis of a destructive or subversive nature,[6] and having distinguished between the supernatural in the Scripture and superstition, he could give his critical reason free rein without feeling any conflict with the exigencies of the revealed faith.

But read within its milieu, Bayle's letter on comets was not even essentially an attack on superstition in general. What is under fire is superstition as it pertains to Catholic belief and practice in France and touches upon Protestant-Catholic differences. And a target of equal importance is the relaxed moral standards of the Catholic society in France. The inspiration of the *Pensées diverses* can more easily be found in partisan religious motives than in a broad philosophic desire to correct popular beliefs.[7]

This view is supported by the account of the book's origin which Bayle set down in 1683 in a letter to Minutoli,[8] who was a professor of Greek and history at the Protestant Academy of Geneva and one of Bayle's closest friends and most trusted confidants. We learn in this letter that while Bayle was in Paris in the early fall of 1680, on business for the Academy of Sedan, he ran into a former classmate with whom he had studied at the college maintained by the Jesuits in Toulouse, and who had just received his doctorate at the Sorbonne. They renewed their acquaintance and reasoned upon "bien des choses," most certainly upon the differences which separated the parties. One of the main subjects of their talks must have been signs, omens, and superstitions, for as a result of their talks, Bayle promised to write his Catholic friend a short dissertation on the subject. The latter asked him to write it as if a Catholic, so that when he showed it to his friends they would not think that he was in correspondence with a heretic.

Several months later, in early December of 1680, the appearance of a large comet furnished Bayle with an excellent opportunity to treat the questions of presages and superstition which had in all likelihood been raised during their conversations. His exhaustive dialectic compelled him to carry every idea to its logical conclusion and led him into such singular conclusions that he hesitated to show the result to anyone. Nonetheless, when Bayle came to Paris in the summer of 1681, shortly after the closing of the Academy of Sedan, he attempted to see his Sorbonne friend but found that he was not in Paris. Bayle therefore kept his manuscript, and after his arrival in Holland in October of the same year, he showed it to a printer who saw that it would sell and started to print it without consulting Bayle, even writing a preface which Bayle retouched when he saw that the work was underway.[9] Bayle had already told the same story to his younger brother, Joseph, stating that the letter on comets had really been intended for, though not delivered to, a Catholic theologian: "Poul la lettre des comètes, je vous avouerai *sub sigillo confessionis* que j'en suis l'auteur. Elle n'a pas été effectivement envoyée à un docteur de Sorbonne, mais j'ai eu en vue un docteur de cette faculté dont le nom répond aux lettres que j'ai fait mettre au titre, avec qui j'ai fait ma philosophie et que je trouvais à Paris il y a deux ans."[10]

The fact that Bayle had in mind a particular Catholic theologian to whom he was writing about Protestant-Catholic differences puts the *Pensées diverses* in a religious context, and shows the seemingly anti-religious remarks in another light. Bayle as a Protestant could criticize many aspects of Catholicism without having the least intention of irreligion. The book is not a completely polemical work, for Bayle put in it his "miscellaneous thoughts" on many subjects, but the core of it is an unmistakable and vigorous challenge to Catholic practice. This is made explicit when the author of the Preface (ostensibly the printer, but in reality Bayle), challenges the Catholic doctor to answer him, saying:

> j'ai su de bonne part que le docteur de Sorbonne à qui cette lettre a été écrite, y prépare une réponse fort exacte et fort travaillée. Il serait fort à craindre, vu son indifférence pour la qualité d'auteur, qu'il ne se contentât de travailler pour son ami si on ne l'engageait, en publiant la lettre qu'il a recue, à faire part au public des belles et savantes réflexions qu'il aura faites. . . . Je m'estimerai fort heureux si je puis être cause que le public . . . voie les réflexions du docteur [sur les matières de cet ouvrage] (*PDC,* p. 5).

It is significant that Bayle challenges the doctor specifically on the very Catholic practices which Protestants had been attacking for over a hundred and fifty years. Such were the extravagant praise of the Virgin and the ridiculous fictions associated with her and the saints, which expose religion "aux insultes et aux railleries de ceux du dehors" (p. 80). In similar manner he condemns the elaborate ceremony and use of ritual employed by some Catholic cardinals (p. 73) and refutes the Catholic argument of antiquity and tradition, which was being invoked against the Protestants, by showing that this argument was not admitted by the Catholics when it was invoked by the pagans (p. 82). He points out that superstition which the Calvinists had attacked without quarter (p. 62), was of pagan origin and had crept into the Primitive Church with false pagan converts (pp. 55–59).

In the same vein, Bayle challenges the doctor to justify the widespread immorality visible in Catholic society by pointing out numerous examples of crime and corruption which are winked at or concealed under the cloak of empty profession (pp. 95–109). Finally, he calls for justification of the current persecution of the "Protestant heresy," by pointing out that a prostitute every day makes the decision that it is better to disobey God's law than to obey it, an action which is certainly very heretical, but she is never bothered because of her heretical decisions. On the other hand, the Huguenots make what the Catholic Church considers errors of speculative theology, which have no relation to morality, and they are subjected to all kinds of oppression (pp. 126–127).

The long digression on atheism in the *Pensées diverses* raises no objection to this interpretation, but rather strengthens it. The digression is based upon Protestant principles and reveals the same element of challenge to Catholic theologians noted above. Far from being an apology for atheism, it is in its context a psychological and theological examination of man and a condemnation of the relaxed Catholic morality. It shows Bayle to be more in harmony with his own age than with the eighteenth century, more in the spirit of Pascal than of Voltaire and the Encyclopedists.

What is the purpose of this digression? Bayle originally sets out to prove that God would not perform miracles among the pagans to keep them from falling into atheism. He supports this assertion by submitting another principle, that atheism is not a worse error than idolatry, which he in turn attempts to prove by maintaining that atheism does not necessarily lead to the corruption of morals. The basis of this last proposition is that belief in future rewards and punishments does not alter men's conduct because man is not reasonable and does not act according to his principles. "Ce ne sont pas les opinions générales de l'esprit qui nous déterminent à agir," insists Bayle in Calvinist fashion, "mais les passions présentes du coeur" (p. 89). He then brings to bear eloquent proof of this natural corruption in man by the examples cited above of multitudes who believe the dogmas of the Church and yet give themselves over to the most serious misconduct (e.g. Christian soldiers, the Crusaders, public women in Rome and Venice, devils and witches, the general run of unregenerated Christians, and numerous criminals who have shown great devotion to the Virgin Mary [pp. 89–96]). Therefore, he concludes, there is no difference morally between an atheist, an idolator, and an unregenerated Christian, because all act from purely human motives and conduct themselves according to their temperament, habit, or dominant passion (p. 93).

Up to this point Bayle's digression has been principally psychological, with occasional asides on Catholic society. The latter now receives the full brunt of his criticism. He cites first Father Rapin, who said there had never been more assiduous attendance at Catholic communion and yet more immorality, after which he also quotes Arnauld who had said that ". . . toutes les véritables marques du christianisme sont presque aujourd'hui éteintes dans les moeurs des chrétiens" (*PDC,* p. 101). Bayle insists that it is in this context that one must consider his conjectures about a society of atheists: "Après toutes ces remarques, je ne ferai pas difficulté de dire, si l'on veut savoir ma conjecture touchant une société d'athées, qu'il me semble qu'à l'égard des moeurs et des actions civiles, elle serait toute semblable à une société de paiens" (*PDC,* p. 103).

It thus becomes clear that in the *Pensées diverses* Bayle is not exalting the atheists, but is rather condemning Christians, for he states that "un esprit superficiel qui m'entendrait raisonner comme je raisonne croirait infailliblement que je fais l'apologie des pécheurs, mais un esprit pénétrant jugerait sans doute que je fais tout le contraire. Car puisque je tâche de prouver que les hommes vivent très mal, quoiqu'ils conservent la persuasion des vérités évangéliques, il est indubitable que je les accuse d'une plus noire méchanceté" (p. 102). It is for this purpose that Bayle undertakes to prove, by citing numerous examples of Parisian life, that the manners of modern Christian society (again, all the examples are drawn from the Catholic milieu) are based on a code of human honor directly opposed to the spirit of the Gospel (pp. 103–110). Now a society of atheists would act according to the very same human motives: desire for glory, desire for honor, and even allegiance to duty (pp. 115–118). In what, he asks, may Christian society claim superiority?

Bayle's intent in writing the digression on atheists becomes clearer in light of certain recent Catholic attacks on the Calvinists. In 1672, the Jansenist Arnauld had written his *Renversement de la morale de Jésus Christ par les erreurs des Calvinistes, touchant la justification,* in which he accused the Calvinists of undermining ethics. By teaching that a sinner could not fall from grace once he had been chosen by God, said Arnauld, the Calvinists weakened the necessity of good works, and they tended also to diminish the fear of divine chastisement in the unregenerate sinner (a fear very useful to society) by teaching that he was irrevocably lost without the grace of God. The ethical doctrine of the Calvinists, insisted Arnauld, was worse than that of the pagans. And the Jesuit Father Adam had gone one step further, charging that the Calvinists made God the Author of sin. It would be better to be an atheist, he said, and recognize no divinity at all than to worship the God of the Calvinists.

Bayle was familiar with these writings, and it becomes clear that when he undertakes to prove that the morals of Catholic France are no different than would be those of a society of atheists, he was trying to hoist the Catholic writers on their own petard.[11]

Nor does Bayle forget the doctor who initially occasioned this torrent of reasonings. Bayle reiterates his challenges and places the doctor in a dilemma. Of course, atheism is "l'état d'une malédiction et d'un abandon qui fait frémir," but a society of atheists would apparently operate from the same motives as most Christian societies. The latter assertion, continues Bayle, is the logical consequence of the doctrine of Original Sin and is thus very contrary to the Pelagian heresy. He therefore calls for the doctor's opinion (*PDC*, p. 123), which would no doubt be "most instructive,"[12] since Bayle's assessment of the moral condition of France would push the theologian either toward Pelagian sentiments or the Calvinist doctrine of grace and predestination, or else force him to agree that most Christians of France were no better than atheists and that the Catholic Church was morally corrupt.

Now it is not quite correct to say, as did Paul Hazard,[13] that Bayle equates idolators, atheists, and all Christians, and that he exalts atheists above the other two, for Bayle repeatedly excepts from his discussion those who are led or sanctified by the Holy Spirit (i.e. the "little flock" of the elect).[14] Although he used a Catholic vocabulary for stylistic purposes (it must be remembered that he was supposedly writing as a Catholic), the Calvinist doctrines of human depravity, grace, and predestination were clearly the basis of the digression on atheism. Man is such a source of evil and corruption, declared Bayle (and the same idea reappears constantly throughout all of his works), that without a divine regeneration, be he atheist, pagan, or Christian, he cannot overcome the passions which dominate his fallen nature (*PDC*, p. 94). It is for this reason, he reiterates, that the pagans, atheists, and unregenerated Christians are on the same footing morally: "La malice des hommes est si prodigieuse qu'il n'y a qu'une grâce particulière du Saint Esprit qui la puisse corriger et ... sans cette grâce, c'est toute la même chose à l'égard des moeurs, ou d'être athée, ou de croire à tous les canons des conciles" (*PDC*, p. 103). Therefore, to discount as precautionary Bayle's idea of grace and the Holy Spirit is to reject as precautionary the very essence of his argument.

Bayle moreover gives his examples of virtuous pagans and atheists only after having distinguished between human virtue, which proceeds from a selfish and human motive, and the virtue of the true Christian, which consists of "la charité, qui nous fait aimer Dieu, et qui nous attache à lui comme à notre souverain bien. . . ." God being the sovereign good, every action of moral worth must be performed for the love of God, and this condition is lacking in the pagans and atheists because in their virtues ". . . il n'y a rien que l'on ne puisse attribuer au tempérament, à l'éducation, au désir de la gloire, au goût que l'on s'est fait pour une sorte de réputation, à l'estime que l'on peut concevoir pour ce qui paraît honnête et louable, et à plusieurs autres motifs qui sont de la compétence de tous les hommes, soit qu'ils aient une religion, soit qu'ils n'en aient pas" (*PDC,* p. 94).

And even when atheists found the idea of disinterested allegiance to the good and the beautiful, as did Seneca and Epicurus, it was not because of their atheism, but because of the action of God upon them, for, Bayle continues, "il faut savoir qu'encore que Dieu ne se révèle pas pleinement à un athée, il ne laisse pas d'agir sur son esprit et de lui conserver cette raison et cette intelligence par laquelle tous les hommes comprennent la vérité des premiers principes de métaphysique et de morales" (PDC, pp. 114–115). If, therefore, Bayle attributed all of the truth and virtue of the atheists to the influence of God, he could hardly have been glorifying or defending atheism.

In addition to showing the Calvinistic basis of Bayle's thinking in 1682, the book of "miscellaneous thoughts" also reveals that there existed in Bayle at this time three different attitudes toward reason. The first was a confidence in reason as a critical tool, marvelously efficient in demolishing the arguments of the adversary, and consequently in defending the true faith. Bayle nonetheless excepted revelation from its scrutiny, but the thought that the two could be in conflict does not seem to have been seriously considered at this time. And the Scripture being silent on the subject of comets and omens, all of the critical powers of reason could be brought to bear.

But man's reason is more than critical. It is the source of a universal moral revelation. It was by this means that the atheists and pagans had discerned the good and the beautiful (pp. 114–115). And Christianity, in Bayle's mind, was the superior religion only because it taught the practice of "des vertus les plus pures et les plus conformes aux lumières de la droite raison. . . ." (p. 121). Serrurier aptly remarked in this regard that "Bayle n'entend pas par la 'lumière naturelle,' la 'raison saine,' le 'bon sens' de Voltaire, mais la conscience morale. . . . Voltaire jugera absurde ce qui est contraire au bon sens, Bayle ne rejette que ce qui est contraire aux bonnes moeurs."[15]

Latent in the *Pensées diverses,* however, is a paradoxical distrust of reason, a growing awareness of its impotence either as a means of discovering truth or as a dominant force in human behavior. In the summary of the *Pensées diverses* Bayle concludes that "il est facile à chacun de s'en convaincre et de voir par le même moyen le tort que nous avons de nous glorifier de notre raison, qui nous est de si peu d'usage que presque tous les hommes se trouvent engagés dans un sentiment destitué de toute sorte de preuves, tant sur la question de droit, que sur la question de fait" (p. 159). The source of this debility is the innate corruption of man which permits the passions to dominate the intellect. As pointed out above, the whole digression on atheists is predicated upon the idea that people do not act according to what they think will be best for them (p. 87), but rather according to their passion or temperament. Belief in the mysteries of Christianity would not be difficult for most people if they were not asked to change their way of life. It is only when they are asked to deny their sensual inclinations that both reason and nature rise in revolt (p. 118). This reservation with regard to reason is here slight, but it was the great gulf which separated Bayle from the *philosophes.* As will be seen, he came to recognize more and more the destructive effects of rational criticism. The effect was to limit reason severely in areas of speculative knowledge and to exalt it in questions of ethics, as in the *Commentaire philosophique.*

Along with the idea of reason stands the idea of grace. For Bayle grace was real and efficacious, but his first writings show that he thought it to be more a moral than an intellectual factor, for it could persuade without enlightening. Christians, he said, are just as given to belief in omens as other people are. The knowledge of God and the Gospel should cure them of that, ". . . mais, hélas! l'homme est toujours l'homme. La Providence divine n'ayant pas trouvé à propos d'établir sa grâce qui soutient notre infirmité. Mais comme le fond de notre nature . . . subsiste toujours, il est moralement impossible que les Chrétiens avec toutes les lumières et toutes les grâces que Dieu répand sur eux, ne tombent dans les mêmes désordres [here, superstition] où tombent les autres hommes" (*PDC,* p. 61). The role of grace, he believed, was to change the disposition and turn one's desires from evil to good, for

> nous avons besoin de l'opération intérieure du St. Esprit afin d'aimer Dieu. Car tout ce que les hommes qui nous instruisent peuvent faire

se réduit à nous persuader de la vérité. Or nous pouvons être persuadés de la vérité sans l'aimer. Donc ce ne sont pas les hommes qui nous font aimer les vérités de l'Evangile; et par conséquent c'est Dieu qui nous les fait aimer, en ajoutant à l'illumination de notre esprit une disposition de coeur qui nous fait trouver plus de joie dans l'exercice de la vertu que dans la pratique du vice (*PDC*, p. 101).

It was this belief in grace which was to form one of the basic elements of Bayle's fideism later on.

One also finds evidence in the *Pensées diverses* that Bayle could see the weaknesses in his own party. He recognized that although the Protestants had attacked the "superstitions of the Papacy," many of them were as infatuated as anyone else with the superstition concerning omens (p. 62). The Reformed Church was then arguing against the Roman claim of antiquity and tradition, but Bayle saw that they would invoke the same argument one day against their own schismatics (p. 82). In short, he recognized a general decline in the Calvinists, who had lost "ce premier feu et cette ardeur qui accompagne tous les grands changements et qui à cause de cela se trouvait dans leurs ancêtres" (p. 58). Significantly, his absence of blind party spirit was probably one of his strongest ties with the Reform. As Rousseau later remarked, one of the real weaknesses of a highly authoritarian system is that the rejection of one part entails the rejection of the whole. It was not so in the Protestant milieu. When Bayle later found himself at odds with the pastor Pierre Jurieu, he could easily find that his former friend and colleague was morally heretical and could denounce him as such without believing himself at all unorthodox.

NOTES

1. Labrousse, *Pierre Bayle*, I, 172.

2. Delvolvé, *Essai*, pp. 44, 51.

3. *La crise de la conscience européenne*, I, 146–147.

4. *PDC, OD*, III, 12.

5. *Essays on Pierre Bayle and Religious Controversy*, pp. 80–120 gives a detailed account of the development of Calvinist rationalism.

6. See Cowdrick, *The Early Reading of Pierre Bayle*, p. 147.

7. This view is also held and developed by Rex, *Essays*, pp. 72–73.

8. It is true that for the third edition of the *Pensées diverses* in 1699 Bayle gave a slightly different version of the book's origin, stating that he had written the work at the insistence of many people who had questioned him about the significance of the large comet which had appeared in December of 1680 and that he had assumed the role of a Catholic in order to obtain official permission to have his work published in the *Mercure galant*. When this permission was not forthcoming, said Bayle, he took the manuscript to

Holland and retained the Catholic style so that no one would suspect that the author was a French refugee. It is important to note, however, that he gave this explanation when, having been accused of taking part in a supposed French-Catholic conspiracy against the Allies and the States of Holland, he had strong motives to play down any relationship he had had with Catholicism or prominent Catholics, which relationship figures prominently in the acount given to Minutoli in 1683. It is therefore not surprising to find that the persecuted philosopher omitted in the 1699 version any reference to the conversations with the Sorbonne doctor which had evidently provided much of the initial inspiration of the book.

9. Letter to Minutoli, 30 March 83, *OD,* IV, 609.

10. 3 October 82, *OD, LFam,* I, 134.

11. These points are made by Rex, in *Essays,* pp. 54–55.

12. Cf. *PDC,* p. 5.

13. See Hazard, *La Crise,* I, 146–147.

14. *PDC,* pp. 88, 94, 104.

15. Serrurier, *Pierre Bayle en Hollande,* pp. 94–95.

6 Reason in Defense of the Faith

IT was not long before Bayle had occasion to answer a challenge himself. In early 1682 the Jesuit Father Maimbourg published his *Histoire du Calvinisme*. Father Maimbourg's intent was to justify the force and temporal measures being used against the recalcitrant Huguenots to dissuade them from their erroneous ways, and one of his chief tactics was to blacken the character of the Reformers and thus to turn public opinion even more against the Reform.

The attack touched Bayle deeply and personally. He had felt the weight of the royal edicts which first separated him from his family and then closed the Academy of Sedan, forcing him into exile for his faith. And even then, while he lived in comparative safety at Rotterdam, he watched the storm gathering over his family and the other Huguenots who still remained in France. "Toutes les nouvelles que nous recevons de France," he wrote to his father, "nous figurent le malheur de l'Eglise le plus triste de la terre. Je tremble quand je songe que vous êtes sous l'autorité d'un parlement qui s'est toujours signalé par sa sévérité contre ceux de la religion, et rien n'est capable de me rassurer que la confiance qu'il faut avoir en cette protection invisible, mais toute puissante que Dieu accorde aux siens."[1] Other letters of this period likewise reflect apprehension and concern for the Protestants in France whose liberties and privileges were inexorably being withdrawn.[2]

Thus, when Bayle read Father Maimbourg's history of Calvinism, he was full of indignation at the Jesuit's "disingenuity and pernicious designs,"[3] and he immediately undertook a formal and major reply entitled *Critique générale de "l'Histoire du Calvinisme."* He finished it in two weeks. One can judge the zeal with which he wrote.

What is first noticeable in the *Critique générale* is the strength of Protestant conviction and commitment which Bayle manifests. He is neither the skeptical nor the impartial and detached onlooker that some critics have seen.[4]

His language, for example, is strong and often denunciatory. If the Catholic Church were judged morally, he asserts, it would be "la plus fausse de toutes les religions" (p. 85).[5] Its use of force is "la plus infernale et la plus exécrable manière de conserver son autorité" (p. 76). Its leaders have governed like the Turks and have sought to submit everything to the "joug de leur barbare domination" (p. 77). The *Critique* is not filled with the railing and high invective of some of the polemical works of the time, but the strong feeling and indignation, though disciplined, are unmistakable.

Bayle gives further proof of his partiality by justifying the excesses of Protestant historians, commenting, for example, that "à l'égard de messieurs des Guise, je conviens avec monsieur du Maurier que plusieurs écrivains protestants ont porté trop loin leurs invectives contre eux: mais on ne me saurait nier que leur préjugé ne fût moins aveugle que celui des écrivains catholiques" (p. 15). He excuses certain intolerant Protestant actions by stating that "la persécution qui nous est faite est plus injuste que le traitement que l'on a fait à l'Eglise romaine dans l'Angleterre," because Louis XIV had promised and then broken his promise, whereas the King of England had never promised anything (pp. 105–106).

Similarly, if he recognizes merit in Catholic writers, it is in those generous to the Protestant cause, such as "Monsieur Maurier . . . qui reconnaît de la fraude dans une infinité de moines et de catholiques superstitieux." Another example is his praise of another Catholic writer, de Thou, in whose writings "vous trouverez la réfutation de M. Maimbourg et l'apologie de notre parti" (p. 67). On the other hand, Bayle is sometimes so anxious to make a point against other Catholic authors that he makes unwarranted assumptions in his arguments, as can be seen in the following statement: "Bon Dieu! que de crimes [attributed to the Protestants in the St. Bartholomew's Massacre] entassés les uns sur les autres! Et que cela nous sert de bonne preuve que toutes les violences qu'on dit que les Huguenots ont faites, sont de pures calomnies, inventées pour colorer et pour pallier la damnable cruauté qu'on exerçait contre le parti!" (p. 85).

The basic ideas and doctrines which appear throughout the *Critique* are uniquely Protestant. Bayle expressed his belief in the inspiration of the Scripture (p. 135), and he declared it to be the sole rule of faith, saying: "Nous voulons un sens de l'Ecriture qui se prouve par l'Ecriture même, et en cela nous faisons voir que nous voulons l'Ecriture pour l'unique règle de notre foi" (p. 71).[6] He also maintained that the Reformers had had ample justification to undertake the task of purifying Christianity, which had become corrupted through immorality and unauthorized additions to its ceremonies and doctrines. Prayers for the dead, he asserted, were "des fadaises" (p. 133); the religion associated with relics and images was criminal (pp. 41, 63, and 81); the Catholic ideas of purgatory were "chimériques et creuses" (p. 68); and the doctrine of Transubstantiation was idolatrous (pp. 133–134). Elsewhere, he declared that Catholicism, in advocating and using force, bribery, and fraud in matters of conscience, had completely turned away from the spirit of Christ and His apostles and had less Christianity in it than the moral precepts of Seneca. In contrast, he saw in the Reformation the pure morality of original Christianity (p. 43). In this connection he made a spirited defense of Calvin's learning and moral character (both of which had been attacked by Maimbourg) and exalted the Genevan as a restorer of the primitive Church (p. 48).

It is perhaps Bayle's stance on the question of Papal infallibility which best shows his confidence in the Reformed doctrine in 1682. As mentioned previously, the authority of the Church was at the basis of the differences of the two parties. Father Maimbourg's justification of the force being used against the Huguenots eventually rested upon the Catholic claim to infallibility, and Bayle consequently set out to refute this dogma, precisely the one which had occasioned his temporary conversion to Catholicism twelve years previously. He had evidently done much thinking on the subject and now maintained that the pretention to infallibility was the least tenable of all Catholic doctrines. It was generally accepted within the Roman confession, said Bayle, only because of the ignorance of the great mass of communicants and because of certain political reasons of the clergy (p. 144). In order to establish this conclusion, he pointed out that for the Catholic Church to be infallible, the question of infallibility would have to be settled independently of the testimony which it bears of itself (p. 121). Now there is no place in the Scripture, he continued, which clearly designates that the Church is to be considered infallible (p. 136). There is not even any statement of the conditions under which the Pope may speak *ex cathedra,* this question itself being the subject of a lively dispute among the theologians of the Roman Church (p. 124). If therefore a layman, who had to be the final judge in any event, could decide these questions, which are among the most difficult, he could decide any others, and thus for Bayle the Protestant principle of free examination was established (p. 136). The Roman Church had therefore erred in the very pretension that it could not err. In contrast to this paradox, Bayle affirmed that the Reformed Church was indeed fallible, but had not erred, stating that "ce qui fait que nous nous soumettons aux décisions de nos synodes, c'est la lumière certaine qu'encore ils se puissent tromper, ils n'ont pas effectivement erré" (p. 145).

One sees in the *Critique,* as in the *Pensées diverses,* that Bayle was conscious of weaknesses in his own party and admitted that "nous avons été attaqués dans un temps où nous avions perdu, par le commerce du monde, cette pureté de sentiments, cette vertu, ces moeurs si corrigées que l'on admirait autrefois au milieu de nous, et à la place de ces divins ornements nous nous étions parés de toutes les passions déréglées de nos concitoyens" (*CG,* p. 102). He still considered that this was not true of the Reformed Church in general. Some Protestant pastors, he said, might like a few more trappings, "mais, Dieu merci, la meilleure partie de nos ministres est encore persuadée qu'on a bien fait de réduire les cultes de la religion à la simplicité apostolique où on les voit parmi nous" (p. 48).

If the *Critique générale* reveals a strong religious conviction and commitment in Bayle in 1682, it also suggests a new direction his thought was taking on the sinuous road leading to the fideism of the *Dictionnaire.*

In answering Maimbourg, Bayle had relied chiefly on the scholastic *ad hominem* argument which refuted an attack by showing that the attacker's own position was vulnerable to the same accusations he was advancing against his opponent. Maimbourg had said that the Protestants had made a Pope of the King of England, to which Bayle replied that the Jesuits had done the same thing with the King of France, making Papal bulls subject to royal approbation (pp. 34–35). When the Jesuit asserted that the Reformed Church could not be true because it was established by violence, his Huguenot opponent countered that if violence were a mark of a false church, there was no true church on the earth during the sixteenth century (p. 36). Again, in reply to the assertion that the Reformed Church could not be true because its founders had been wicked, Bayle denied that they had been wicked and then pointed out that if corrupt morals were a mark of false doctrine, the Catholic Church had fallen into apostasy long ago (p. 69). And when Maimbourg advanced the familiar argument that the Reformation could not be true, because the Catholic Church was the old and traditional church, Bayle answered simply that "nous n'avons qu'à lâcher contre eux le paganisme armé de leurs lieux communs, et nous les verrons périr par leurs propres armes" (p. 87). In a word, he warned, "il faut être en état de ne pas craindre la rétorsion, quand on ose reprocher aux protestants les irrégularités que l'on croit voir dans les manières de leur Réforme" (p. 129).

In this manner, Bayle had completely disarmed his opponent, who found himself obliged either to abandon his attack or deny his Catholic position.[7] Nevertheless, Bayle recognized that critical reason was a two-edged sword which sometimes did as much mischief to the Protestant cause as to the Catholic, in which event he also was compelled either to deny his Protestant position or else deny the authority of reason. In the *Critique* he recognized, for example, that according to the dictates of reason, God should surely have established an infallible Church and clothed it with incontestable marks of truth so that no one could mistake it, but since the evidence led him to believe that such was not the case, he was forced to invoke the inscrutability of God's ways, saying: "Comme je l'ai dit ci-dessus, il y a une distance infinie entre ce qui est sagesse à l'égard de l'homme et ce qui est sagesse à l'égard de Dieu. Il ne faut pas s'étonner que Dieu ait laissé son Eglise exposée aux divisions et aux hérésies, après tant de choses qui nous surprennent dans l'enchaînure des choses" (p. 143).

Significantly, he was also becoming more and more aware that the only danger to the Protestant faith was not in the Catholic attacks. A growing number of libertines, deists, and atheists represented a threat to all confessions. The ground was becoming slippery, and Bayle here foreshadowed the moment when the religious person could no longer argue on rational grounds: "En effet, la nature divine étant infinie en toutes ses perfections, il faut nécessairement que la sagesse avec laquelle Dieu gouverne toutes choses soit infinie, et par conséquent incompréhensible à l'homme." One should not expect, therefore, that "la Providence de Dieu s'est imposée les mêmes bornes et les mêmes règles que la prudence humaine est obligée de garder" (p. 128).

It would be supposed that for one who reasoned as keenly as did Bayle, this recourse to the incomprehensible would automatically amount to a negation of religious belief. However, his mind and background, as has been shown previously, were much more complex. Cartesian evidence might well be the condition of *proof* in a dispute, but his concept of conscience and faith did not make rational satisfaction a necessary condition to personal belief. He attached considerable importance to the idea that since the workings of Providence were infinite, they could not, by definition, be understood by finite reason. In addition, though believing the Scripture to be the rule of faith, he believed that faith in it depended on grace. He gave an indication of his belief in divine and supra-rational influence in a remark condemning the use of force in matters of conscience: "[Les Catholiques voulurent] avoir plus d'empire sur la conscience que Dieu lui-même n'en prend; Dieu, dis-je, qui étant le maître absolu de toutes choses se dépouille entièrement, selon la théologie de ces messieurs, de son autorité sur notre âme afin de lui laisser son franc arbitre tout entier; et selon nous [les calvinistes] il ne conduit notre âme où il la veut que par des inflexions douces et bénignes" (*CG,* p. 76). This is in accord with the assertion which recurs several times in the *Critique,* that conscience (and thus, belief) depends on God alone (pp. 77 and 91). It was thus possible for a reasoner who believed in the inadequacy of reason to subject reason to belief in the incomprehensible, especially since he believed that morality was the most important part of religion and the principal mark of the true faith.

But Bayle did not push these ideas to their logical conclusion in the *Critique générale.* He apparently did not yet believe the gap between faith and reason to be unbridgeable, and his contemporaries in orthodox Protestant circles in Holland considered him to be nothing less than a defender of the faith. When Father Maimbourg's *Histoire du calvinisme* had appeared, all of the Protestant camp waited anxiously for some David to answer the threats and violence of this new Goliath, and the *Critique générale* fulfilled all of their hopes and expectations. Since Bayle published this work anonymously, it was attributed to some of the foremost Protestant spokesmen, including the ministers Claude and Jurieu. The latter did indeed write his own answer to Maimbourg several months later, answering the Jesuit on every point, but the public apparently continued to prefer Bayle's work to Jurieu's reply.[8] Nor were the *Pensées diverses* esteemed less highly than the *Critique.* The book on comets enjoyed a great success in Protestant circles and raised no immediate question as to the orthodoxy of its author.[9] To the contrary, on the strength of Bayle's reputation as author of the *Pensées diverses,* the Protestant Academy of Franecker offered him a chair in philosophy in early 1684 (which he declined).[10]

The first eighteen months that Bayle spent in Rotterdam saw him rise from obscurity and acquire a reputation as one of the foremost Protestant authors. His circle of acquaintances widened, and he entered into a voluminous correspondence with learned people throughout Europe. His reputation was further enhanced by his monthly journal *Les Nouvelles de la République des Lettres,* which he started to write in 1684, consisting of summaries and critiques of forthcoming books. He was officially praised by the French Academy, The Royal Society of London, and The Royal Society of Ireland. His interests remained wide in things erudite, but it was religious controversy which occupied an increasing proportion of his attention and energy, and it was the pressures and stresses of religious controversy which were to make the years 1684–87 the most crucial in his intellectual development.

NOTES

1. 26 March 82, *LFam, OD,* I, 130.

2. See letters to his father, 1 April 79, *NL,* II, 88–89; 4 Feb 80, *LFam, OD,* I, 121; 28 Oct. 80, *LFam, OD,* I, 124.

3. Des Maizeaux, "Life of Bayle," p. xvi.

4. Delvolvé, *Eassai,* pp. 55, and Serrurier, *Pierre Bayle en Hollande,* pp. 68–69.

5. All quotations from the *Critique générale* are found in the *Oeuvres diverses,* Vol. II.

6. It is also revealing that at this time (1682) he interpreted the famous *compelle intrare* parable in Luke and tried to show how the Catholics had not understood it. He later (*ca.* 1686) recognized, however, that the problems of Scriptural interpretation rendered such exegesis futile. See *CG, OD,* II, p. 94.

7. *CG, OD,* II, p. 37. See also pp. 48–49, 63, 83, 98.

8. The Jesuit Father chose the former course and did not attempt to answer the Protestant professor. He did, however, obtain the suppression of the *Critique* in France, a circumstance which naturally increased its popularity and augmented the reputation of its author. See Des Maizeaux, "Life of Bayle," p. xvi.

9. See Des Maizeaux, "Life of Bayle," p. xvi.

10. It was only in 1693 that Jurieu, motivated by a personal grudge, accused the author of the *Pensées diverses* of atheism. See Rex, *Essays,* pp. 72–73, and Labrousse, "Documents relatifs à l'offre d'une chaire de philosophie à Bayle à l'Université de Franeker au printemps de 1684," in *Pierre Bayle, le philosophe de Rotterdam,* p. 220, for a further description of Protestant reaction to the *Pensées diverses.*

7 Reason vs. Faith

ONE of the fascinating things about seventeenth-century controversy is the way in which the titles grow. A "Treatise" is followed by "An Answer to the Impertinent Treatise . . . " which calls forth a "Refutation of the Infamous Answer to the Treatise . . . . " which in turn provokes "An Examination, which Completely Demolishes the Specious Refutation of the Answer to the Treatise . . . " There is something virile and confident about such disputation. One senses that each author is completely sure of the truth and of his ability to convince any honest seeker.

But somehow the dispute never ends. The expectation of victory never materializes, and as the disputants attempt to end the controversy, the ground shifts. New arguments appear, and the slippery path leads to unexpected destinations.

It is this spirit and course that characterized the three-way battle royal in France between the Catholics (including both the Jesuits and Jansenists, who had sharply disputed with each other), the Protestants (principally Calvinists) and also heterodox rationalists (e.g. Socinians and Spinozists). But instead of establishing truth by their mutual attacks, they only succeeded in revealing their respective weaknesses to the onlookers, that is, the small but growing number of libertines, deists, and atheists.

Their inter- and intraconfessional controversies were all the more destructive because all of their differences ultimately came back to the question of the *analyse de la foi,* i.e., the rule of faith, the ultimate authority in matters of belief, the foundation upon which each party rested. Each party hoped, naturally, that reason, the Scripture, and the church hierarchy would all agree with each other, but if they did not, which one would rule the others? Which one was the most credible and furnished the most solid basis for belief? The effect of the religious controversy was to show that none of them was conclusive.

One of the most persistent Catholic charges was that the Reformers were schismatics, and it was the one most vigorously rejected.[1] In 1684 the Jansenist Nicole thought he had found the way to make it stick. Imbued with Cartesianism, he advanced the thesis in his *Les Prétendus Réformés convaincus de schisme* that even if the first Reformers had been right in their contentions, they would still have been schismatic in separating from the Roman Church because they could not have known demonstrably that they were right.

Nicole's book represented a challenge which Bayle felt compelled to answer. First of all, as editor of the *Nouvelles de la République des Lettres* he had assumed a unique role. He was to be first a "historian," faithfully summarizing the contents of the books he reviewed. He was thus obligated to read and become familiar with all the forthcoming books which were available to him. In addition, he was to be a commentator, or judge, giving an evaluation of his authors' reasoning and conclusions, irrespective of party considerations. "Il ne s'agit point ici de religion," Bayle had declared, "il s'agit de science."[2] Given this public commitment and the qualities of his mind, he doubtless felt that anything less than a full and complete confrontation of the issue would not have been intellectually honest.

But a more cogent reason for answering Nicole was that the interests of the Protestant cause required it, and Bayle was vitally concerned with those interests. Promises of fairness and objectivity in his journal did not mean neutrality — he praised Catholic and Protestant authors alike,[3] but he did not scruple to attack the doctrines of Infallibility[4] and Transubstantiation,[5] to refute accusations leveled at the Protestants by Catholic writers,[6] or to riddle with irony any book attempting to deny or justify the current persecution of the Huguenots.[7] He saw the effects of Catholic intolerance on his friends and family still in France[8] and not to have answered Nicole would have lent justification to it.

But *how* was this new kind of attack to be answered? Could one meet the challenge by showing clearly and demonstrably that the first Reformers really had been right? In short, could the answer be made on rational grounds?

As has been pointed out previously, there was a strong element of rationalism in French Calvinism. The very basis of the Protestant faith was the belief that every person should examine the Scripture for himself and stand as the final judge of its interpretation (a principle very much akin to Descartes' method), and Bayle had been in sympathy with the efforts of Christian philosophers to make Christianity a rational theology. He had said in the *Pensées diverses* (1682) that he was not far removed from the ideas of Malebranche,[9] and the Catholic father's efforts to harmonize the principles of Cartesianism with orthodox Christianity had exercised an enormous influence on Bayle's thinking, an influence very evident in Part I of the *Commentaire philosophique*.[10]

But the publication of Nicole's book, insignificant in itself, was one of the catalysts of Bayle's intellectual development. It may not have been the first time that Bayle had thought about the potential danger which the Cartesian method represented to questions of faith, but never before had he had to confront the issues so squarely, and he now saw clearly the implications of trying to prove religion rationally. In reviewing Nicole's book he saw that it would be easy enough to retort this argument by showing the Catholics to be vulnerable to the same objection, but this procedure, in his view, would only destroy both parties. In short, if Cartesian certainty were required in all things, "ce principe serait *l'éponge de toutes les religions*."[11]

It is capital for the understanding of Bayle's thought to realize that he did not choose to abandon faith by fighting the battle on the terms of the rationalists, although many critics have maintained that he was a rationalist.[12] During the last half of 1684 he seems to have been making his own pre-Kantian critique of pure reason which convinced him that reason was incapable of dealing with the problems of theology and philosophy.

A concept old in Calvinism and Christianity, that human nature and reason, because of the Fall, were dominated by the passions, inclined him to this assessment of reason. In the *Nouvelles Lettres critiques* (1684), (the same work in which he answered Nicole), he digressed at length to prove that even though reason in man's fallen state could reveal the basic precepts of morality,[13] it (reason) was of so little effect in regulating conduct that humanity would perish in a short time if Providence did not utilize man's passions for its own ends (*NLC*, pp. 271–279). In another digression in the same work, he declared that the same corruption which made reason so imperfect as a moral influence also made it imperfect as an intellectual guide, for according to Bayle, "nous n'agissons que par préjugé, que par instinct, que par amour propre, et que par les ressorts de mille passions qui entraînent et qui tournent notre raison comme bon leur semble, de sorte qu'on pourrait très justement définir le principe qui nous règle et qui nous domine, *un amas de préjugés qui sait tirer des conséquences*" (*NLC*, p. 328).

Were not the more astute philosophers and scholars exempt from this general fallibility? His periodical is replete with observations on human imperfection which had caused the most capable of savants to fall into gross error. One such is in the review of a book showing the progress of the fable of Romulus, where he commented:

> Une des plus grandes marques de l'infirmité de l'homme est que plus il acquiert de connaissances, plus il trouve qu'il n'y a presque rien de certain. Jamais la philosophie n'a été plus près de sa perfection qu'en ce siècle, et c'est à présent que l'on est plus convaincu que jamais qu'on ne nous débite que des jeux d'imagination plus ou moins heureux, mais toujours très incertains. L'histoire n'est pas exempte de cette disgrâce, car plus on l'étudie, plus on en connaît l'incertitude.[14]

Jansenism, he observed on another occasion, had been the subject of fierce controversy among the most learned men in France, but it was only a figment of the imagination, because the famous five propositions of Jansenius which had been condemned by the Pope in 1640 and combatted since then by the Jesuits had been disavowed by the Jansenists themselves. He therefore concluded that ". . . on a beau se remplir en général de l'histoire du jansénisme, on ne laisse pas d'en négliger le plus important, qui est d'y connaître la vanité et la sottise de l'homme.[15]

Bayle's evaluation of the powers of reason, however, was based on more than the Calvinist doctrine of human corruption. The decisive factor in his subjection of reason to faith was his conclusion, which was reached while scrutinizing the arguments of the heterodox rationalists, that all rational investigation of theological or philosophical questions eventually yields, not clarity and evidence, but rather antinomies which render reason powerless either to affirm or deny. Significantly, it was in weighing the arguments of an anonymous Socinian book entitled *Religio rationalis* in September, 1684, that he first stated clearly and unmistakably that reason was not competent to pronounce judgment upon questions of speculative knowledge.

The thesis of the book was that any interpretation of the Scripture which contradicted the light of reason should be rejected. Bayle recognized the general difficulty of the problem, but he insisted that the author of the book in question had not proved this thesis, for, according to Bayle,

> il fallait prouver que *la raison est tellement la règle de notre foi qu'il ne faut jamais croire comme révélé de Dieu que ce qui est conforme aux maximes de la raison et à l'expérience de la nature.* Mais c'est ce qu'il ne prouve pas et qu'il ne prouvera jamais . . . [L'auteur] a bien vu que pour raisonner conséquemment a ses principes, il doit rejeter comme faux tout ce que la raison ne saurait comprendre; ainsi il nie

que Dieu ait fait le monde de rien. Mais comme il ne peut pas nier que Dieu n'ait été de tout temps, autre doctrine absolument incompréhensible quant à la manière, il s'échappe en trois mots et dit que la raison s'accorde fort bien à cela, puisqu'elle montre qu'il est nécessaire que la première de toutes les causes n'ait point de commencement. Pour peu qu'on sache ce que c'est que de raisonner et de disputer, on sent que cette objection demeure victorieuse; car puisque la raison nous prouve nécessairement l'existence d'une chose incompréhensible, il s'ensuit qu'il y a des choses très vraies et très réelles qui sont incompréhensibles à la raison, et dès là, tous les arguments des sociniens, empruntés du lieu commun de l'incompréhensibilité, n'ont aucune force.[16]

The next month, in October 1684, Bayle again elaborated on the theme that human understanding was not capable of sounding the depths of either religion or philosophy. An anonymous author had written a book entitled *L'Impie convaincu* in which he presented some strong arguments against the systems of both Spinoza and Descartes. Bayle discounted the arguments against Descartes as only apparent, insisting that "il ne faut pas s'imaginer pour toutes ces grandes difficultés que le cartésianisme soit faux, car de la manière que notre esprit est conditionné, il trouve souvent des embarras insurmontables, quoi qu'il fasse, soit qu'il nie, soit qu'il affirme."[17] In other words, because finite reason could never understand the infinite and eternal, it could always find obscurities and hence possible objections in any system which pretended to explain the infinite and eternal, whether that system were false or true. Reason was therefore more fit to destroy than to build up, and for Bayle all that it revealed clearly and conclusively was its own impotence. He obviously could not answer the challenge of rationalism by showing by clear and evident principles of reason that the Protestants had been justified in separating from the Roman Church.

Could he not invoke the authority of the Scripture, if reason were so fallible? The same polemical activities which had moved him to make his critique of reason also made him aware of certain limitations in the Scripture. In the first place, it became increasingly evident that there was no infallible rule for interpreting the sacred text. On most points the Calvinists could hold for a literal interpretation, and in 1682 Bayle had reproached the Catholics in the *Critique générale* for having made the Scripture subject to their opinions rather than making their opinions subject to the Scripture (*CG,* p. 135). But in the same work Bayle had to reverse his stand when discussing the doctrine of Transubstantiation and say that reason had to interpret any passage where a literal meaning was impossible (*CG,* p. 134), and this procedure entailed all of the difficulties which attended a rational exegesis.

In 1684 Bayle was still more conscious that the meaning of the Scripture was not unequivocal. It was not possible, for instance, to justify one's actions by citing the example of Biblical personages, many of these being, in Bayle's view, morally reprehensible. Even such famous women as Sarah, Leah, and Rachel were not models of virtue, for they had prostituted their servants to their husbands for no other reason than the ridiculous and selfish shame of being sterile (*NLC,* p. 274). Recently a Cardinal Baronius had tried to justify his use of strong language and his approval of violence by citing incontestable examples from the Scripture — Peter, Elijah, Phineas, Moses, and John the Baptist, and yet, commented Bayle, ". . . si la patience et la débonnaireté ne sont point clairement commandées dans l'Ecriture, quelle chose pourra passer pour claire? Et qu'est-ce qu'un pyrrhonien ne ruinera pas par les propres armes de l'Ecriture?"

Bayle for his own count was not skeptical on the point, but to prove he was right to a determined opponent was another question. The Apostles were inspired, he said, but we are in "cet état de connaissance mêlé d'obscurités [où] le plus sûr pour nous est sans doute de nous ranger au chemin battu de l'Evangile qui est celui de la douceur et de la modération."[18]

In addition, the growing science of textual criticism had created other difficulties. The findings of such Protestant critics as Cappel and Grotius, or of such notorious unbelievers as Hobbes and Spinoza had forced reappraisal of the prevailing notions concerning the completeness and accuracy of the Biblical text, without, however, posing a grave threat to the orthodox faith. It was only after 1678 when the Catholic Father Richard Simon published his *Histoire critique du Vieux Testament* that the limitations of the Scripture became evident. By showing that Moses could not have written all of the books attributed to him, that parts of the Old Testament are only abridgements of longer works now lost, that there existed no uncorrupted text, and that there was extant no correct translation of the existing manuscripts, Father Simon had demonstrated to his contemporaries, whether intentionally or not, that appeal to the Scripture could not put an end to controversy.[19]

The attitude of John Dryden is revealing in this connection, for he wrote his poem *Religio Laici* (1682), in part at least, in response to the challenge of Simon's *Histoire critique,* which had appeared in English translation in early 1682. Dryden admitted, as all were obliged to do in face of the evidence, that the Biblical text had undergone change, and although he maintained that for himself the basic articles of faith were "few and plain" (line 432), he concluded that the Scripture could not be an infallible authority in settling religious disputes. If it were subject to private interpretation, he remarked, its obscurities resulted in ecclesiastical anarchy:

> A thousand daily sects rise up and die;
> A thousand more the perished race supply:
> So all we make of Heaven's discover'd will
> Is, not to have it, or to use it ill.

(lines 421–424)

On the other hand, he disclaimed the Roman interpretation by tradition, noting that if the sacred text had been altered, no councils nor theologians could reveal its meaning,

> Unless like Esdras they could write it new:
> Strange confidence, still to interpret true,
> Yet not be sure that all they have explain'd,
> Is in the blest original contain'd.

(lines 292–294)

It is certain that Bayle was also considerably influenced by Father Simon. In spite of the vast differences in their backgrounds, they both shared a common respect for facts and for the truth above the considerations of party spirit, and Bayle felt an affinity for some of Simon's methods and principles.[20] It should be noted, too, that the only real examination of the Scriptural text to be found in Bayle's *Dictionnaire* — in the famous article "David" — owed its principles directly to Father Simon.[21]

Bayle had become completely familiar with Simon's work by 1684,[22] and it is more than probable that he was already cognizant of difficulties which textual criticism posed to Scriptural exegetes. In any event, by mid-1686 when he wrote the *Commentaire philosophique* he was convinced that no speculative doctrine could be irrefutably established by the Scripture, for he declared:

> Il n'est pas possible d'arriver à une telle idée, à l'égard de ce seul point de fait, qu'un tel passage de l'Ecriture a été bien traduit, que le mot qui est aujourd'hui dans le grec ou dans l'hébreu y a toujours été et que le sens que lui ont donné les paraphrastes, les commentateurs, et les traducteurs, est le même que celui de l'auteur du livre. On peut avoir une certitude morale de cela, et fondée sur de très grandes probabilités, mais au fond cette certitude se peut rencontrer dans l'âme d'une infinité de gens qui se trompent; ainsi elle n'est pas un caractère certain de la vérité.[23]

It is important to emphasize at this juncture that in spite of admitting that the Scriptural text was not perfect enough to *prove* any particular doctrine to be true, Bayle personally, like Dryden and Simon himself, did not cease to believe in the Scripture. He was not among those of the Reformed Church who, believing that every line and word of the Bible was inspired, were easily shaken by the suggestion that there might have been textual alterations. In reviewing the fifth edition of Simon's *Histoire critique du Vieux Testament* (in late 1684), Bayle said: "Je ne sais si l'on ne pourrait pas dire qu'il y a certaines matières si délicates que pour peu que l'on y touche, l'on jette l'alarme dans les esprits." The fear was needless, he continued, for the same thing had happened when Saint Jerome started to revise the Bible, and he was later recognized to have been raised up by God to do the task. Everyone had eventually realized that there were errors in the Vulgate text, and this had not affected the Protestants more than the Catholics.[24]

As a matter of fact, Bayle had himself been taught liberal principles of exegesis at Geneva by Tronchin,[25] and this early training permitted him to believe in the Scripture even though it did not have a perfect text. Consequently, Bayle was not unduly disturbed by textual variations, for in 1685, while commenting on the prospectus of a polyglot Bible which might show errors in the Scriptural text, he said:

> Ce n'est point la doctrine des protestants que chaque livre, chaque chapitre, et chaque verset de l'Ecriture soit la base et la règle de la religion. En effet, quand on leur objecte qu'il y a des citations dans la Bible qu'on ne trouve plus et qu'on en infère qu'il s'est perdu quelque livre canonique, ils ne font pas de difficulté d'avouer que quand cela serait vrai, leur foi n'en recevrait point de préjudice, parce que les vérités nécessaires au salut se trouvent assez clairement contenues dans ce qui nous reste. Il faut dire la même chose touchant les petites altérations qu'on prétend qui se sont glissées dans le texte de l'Ecriture ... le corps des vérités révélées n'est pas attaché à cinq ou six voyelles ou consonnes; il est répandu dans tout le canon.[26]

But throughout Bayle's writings, and especially in the *Dictionnaire,* there is a trenchant condemnation of the immoral actions of certain Biblical saints and heroes. Is this not an attempt to undermine the authority of the Scripture?

In criticizing the personal morality of Biblical personages Bayle was not rejecting the inspiration of the Bible. In reality, he was only following in the footsteps of presumably the most orthodox of all Calvinists, that is, of Calvin himself. Abraham, Calvin had said, was to be severely blamed because of his subterfuges in Egypt, for he had overstepped the bounds set by the Almighty and had not committed the outcome to God.[27] Lot also was a holy man, who risked his own life in defense of his guests. Yet, maintained Calvin, he was reprehensible in offering his daughters to the mob: ". . . he should rather have endured a thousand deaths, than to have resorted to such a measure. Yet such are commonly the works of holy men: since nothing proceeds from them so excellent, as not to be in some respect defective . . . he is not free from blame because we would ward off evil with evil."[28] Bayle, in commenting upon Calvin's stand, said that he (Calvin) was only making free use of the right ". . . que la raison et l'Ecriture nous donnent de prononcer sur la qualité d'une action," for this was incomparably more useful to Christian morality than all of the expedients of the Fathers to justify Abraham's conduct.[29] This was the same principle Bayle was to follow in writing his article on David: individuals have the right to judge the moral value of an action when the Scripture does not specifically say that it was inspired by the Holy Ghost.[30]

In short, by the time Bayle undertook in late 1684 to answer Nicole's attack on the Reformed Church, he had concluded that neither the dictates of reason nor exegesis of the Scripture could answer the questions of theology and philosophy clearly and demonstrably. The way of examination had promised certainty and had brought him to the edge of skepticism.

But the Huguenot philosopher's background furnished another basis for belief. Rather than reject the mysteries of the orthodox faith or succumb to the indifference of doubt, Bayle chose to follow the subjective way of grace and make the dictates of conscience the supreme standard of belief, and on this basis he remained firmly in the Reformed Church. He made his position explicit in the course of a long digression in the *Nouvelles Lettres critiques* where in specific answer to Nicole he again emphasized the danger which the maxims of Descartes represented for Christianity as a whole, and predicted that if the Protestants and Catholics both insisted that the other establish its principles with the degree of evidence required by Descartes' method, both would be destroyed, and the field would be left to the libertines and deists (*NLC,* p. 334).

It was urgent, then, that an antidote be found for the acid of Cartesian reason which would consume not only the infected part of a wound, but, from the orthodox point of view, the living flesh and bone as well. Bayle felt that he had found such an antidote in the principle that ". . . *en matière de religion il ne faut point suspendre son consentement jusqu'à ce que l'on ait acquis toute l'évidence qu'on attend dans la philosophie de Monsieur Descartes avant de prendre parti.*"

In stating this principle, however, he was in reality removing religion from the realm of rational investigation and making belief dependent upon subjective factors, for he continued:

> Pour établir ce principe, il en faut poser un second, à peu près tel que celui-ci, qu'en *matière de religion, la règle de juger n'est point dans l'entendement, mais dans la conscience;* c'est-à-dire, qu'il faut embrasser les objets non pas selon des idées claires et distinctes, acquises par un examen sévère, mais selon que la conscience nous dicte qu'en les embrassant nous ferons ce qui est agréable à Dieu. Il en faut venir là nécessairement, tant parce que la foi que le Saint Esprit nous communique nous remplit d'une pleine persuasion sans l'aide d'un long examen, que parce que si on voulait s'en tenir aux lumières de l'entendement, il ne faudrait pas embrasser les dogmes d'une religion sans avoir observé tous les préceptes de Monsieur Descartes. Or c'est une chose qui surpasse les forces de presque tous les chrétiens et qui ne saurait être nécessaire sans qu'il s'ensuivît que de dix mille chrétiens il n'y en a pas deux qui croient autrement que par une témérité criminelle" (*NLC*, p. 334).

Believing that reason itself was a fallible guide and being convinced of the reality of grace which enlightened the conscience and gave a full persuasion of the truth without a long and rigorous examination, Bayle could in all honesty subject reason to faith and protest as he did later in his *Dictionnaire* that "... il n'y a point de contradiction entre ces deux choses: (1) la lumiére de la raison m'apprend que cela est faux; (2) je le crois pourtant parce que je suis persuadé que cette lumière n'est pas infaillible et parce que j'aime mieux déférer aux preuves de sentiment et aux impressions de la conscience, en un mot à la parole de Dieu, qu'à une démonstration métaphysique."[31]

He well realized, however, the import of having recourse to grace in a controversy. A little more than a year later when the pastor Jurieu in his *Vrai Système de l'Eglise* (1686) also undertook to answer the arguments Nicole had advanced in his book *Les Prétendus réformés convaincus de schisme,* he (Jurieu) was forced to make scriptural interpretation depend upon a subjective *examen d'attention,* during which the Holy Spirit would enlighten the mind of the reader. Bayle did not fail to see that Jurieu had made the great avowal "qui fait quitter le terrain aux ministres," for it submitted the Scripture to a subjective authority and rendered impossible any objective and conclusive interpretation of its meaning.[32] The gap between faith and reason was yawning wider.

NOTES

1. See Rex, *Essays,* pp. 4–7, and Labrousse, *Pierre Bayle,* I, 68–72.

2. Preface to the *NRL, OD,* I, 2.

3. See *NRL,* March 1684, p. 22; July 1684, p. 100; July 1685, pp. 333–335; November 1685, pp. 421–422; March 1686, pp. 510–511.

4. *NRL,* May 1684, p. 47; October 1686, p. 657; December 1686, pp. 700, 713.

5. *NRL,* April 1684, p. 46; June 1686, p. 581; December 1686, p. 713.

6. See his review of another work by Maimbourg, *Histoire de la Ligue,* in *NRL,* April 1684, pp. 27–30.

7. Some of the more prominent examples are found in *NRL,* July 1685, p. 333; August 1685, p. 356; December 1685, pp. 433, 442; February 1686, pp. 485, 495; March 1686, pp. 517, 522; April 1686, pp. 541, 545; May 1686, pp. 554–555; June 1686, pp. 576, 587; July 1686, pp. 602, 606; August 1686, pp. 611–614; November 1686, p. 689; December 1686, p. 713.

8. See letter to his younger brother, 9 July 82, *LFam, OD,* I, 133, and letter to his older brother, 12 April 83, *LFam, OD,* I, 136. See also the letter from Jacob Bayle to Pierre Bayle, 12 May 85, in Gigas, *Correspondence,* pp. 171–173.

9. *PDC, OD,* III, 130.

10. See Rex, *Essays,* pp. 153–155. See also *NRL,* August 1684, p. 104.

11. *NRL,* November 1684, p. 161.

12. See Robinson, *Bayle the Sceptic,* p. 87, and Hazard, *La Crise,* pp. 94–95.

13. *NLC, OD,* II, 282. It was in fact the doctrine of Original Sin which served as a counterbalance to the strong emphasis on reason in Calvinism. See Rex, *Essays,* pp. 156–157.

14. *NRL,* December 1684, p. 185.

15. *NRL,* January 1687, p. 740.

16. *NRL,* September 1684, pp. 132–133.

17. *NRL,* October 1684, p. 157.

18. *NLC,* pp. 197–198. For other examples of Bayle recognizing obscurities in the Scripture, see *NLC,* p. 208; *NRL,* July 1686, pp. 592–594.

19. For an account of Father Simon's influence on the learned world of the time, see Louis Bredvold, *The Intellectual Milieu of John Dryden* (Ann Arbor, Michigan, 1934), pp. 98–107.

20. *NRL,* November 1685, p. 422.

21. Actually, this bit of criticism which contributed no little to Bayle's reputation for irreligion was in reality aimed at the faulty chronology of David's life in Moréri's dictionary. Bayle was simply pointing out that even though many people hesitated to suspect that the Biblical text had been changed as had certain other ancient texts, there were still obvious inaccuracies in Biblical chronology which Moréri had not corrected. Moréri had reported David as having spared Saul's life two times, whereas, said Bayle, this was only the same event reported two times, and he then cited Simon as his authority, saying: "Je laisse à Monsieur Simon et à des critiques de sa volée à examiner s'il serait possible que les livres historiques du Vieux Testament reportassent deux fois la même chose." *DHC,* "David," note K (1697), I, 930. See also note C, p. 924.

22. See *NRL,* December 1684, p. 191.

23. *CP, OD,* II, 438.

24. *NRL,* December 1684, pp. 191–192.

25. See Antoine Adam, *Histoire de la littérature française au XVIIe siècle* (Paris, 1956), V, 231.

26. *NRL,* January 1685, p. 211.

27. John Calvin, *Commentaries on the First Book of Moses called Genesis,* trans. John King (Grand Rapids, Michigan, 1948), I, 359–360.

28. Calvin, *Commentaries,* I, 500.

29. *DHC,* "Sara," note I, IV, 2539–2540.

30. *DHC,* "David," note I, II, 967.

31. *DHC,* "Spinoza," note H, 1st ed. (1697), II, 1090.

32. *NRL,* April 1686, pp. 527-528.

8   Faith and Intolerance

WHILE Bayle was studying under Tronchin at Geneva, he had found Descartes' principles to be a formidable ally in attacking the Catholic view of the Eucharist. Now Nicole had turned the Cartesian method against the Calvinists, and it had become evident to Bayle that reason was a two-edged sword. Nicole's attack had had the effect of dividing reason and revelation in Bayle's mind, showing that they did not always complement each other and were often inimical. But even though the question Nicole had treated was momentous, it was still basically speculative, since it did not have an immediate ethical effect. In 1685, as a prelude and postlude to the Revocation of The Edict of Nantes, the inter-confessional controversies took another turn and started to revolve more and more around the question of tolerance and the use of force in matters of belief. Here the question was immediate, and its solution was imperative. And it was just when Bayle was concluding that the Scripture was not susceptible of any conclusive exegesis that he found himself in the necessity of interpreting a passage of the New Testament, or more exactly, refuting an interpretation that had been given of it.

The text was Jesus' parable of the wedding supper during which the master of the house said to his servant, "Go out into the highways and hedges and compel them to come in, that my house may be filled" (Luke 14:23). St. Augustine had cited this parable to justify the use of force in bringing the heretical Donatists back into the orthodox fold during the fourth century, and now the Archbishop of Paris had cited both St. Augustine and Christ's parable to justify the use of force in bringing the heretical Protestants back into the Catholic Church. His work, entitled *La Conformité de la conduite de l'Eglise de France pour ramener les donatistes à l'Eglise catholique,* appeared in 1685. The archbishop was not the first to cite the parable but his work, appearing just previous to the Revocation of the Edict of Nantes, was the most significant and was soon followed by works of other Catholic writers who proceeded to cite St. Augustine in defense of the measures taken against the Huguenots to "compel them to come in."[1]

For Bayle, such reasoning was pernicious — in November of 1685 his brother Jacob, a pastor, died in a dungeon at the hands of those seeking to bring about his "conversion." In February, 1686, Pierre released part of his pent-up indignation by writing a short work entitled *Ce que c'est que la France toute catholique sous le règne de Louis le Grand.* Here he proclaimed that the controversy between Christians could only discredit Christianity intellectually in the eyes of the irreligious rationalists and that the use of force against the Protestants would make Christianity a "stench in the nostrils of all nations."[2] But he recognized that such denunciations did not refute the arguments advanced by his opponents, for which purpose he undertook to write his *Commentaire philosophique sur ces paroles de Jésus-Christ: Contrains-les d'entrer; où l'on prouve par plusieurs raisons démonstratives qu'il n'y a rien de plus abominable que de faire des conversions par la contrainte, et où l'on réfute tous les sophismes des convertisseurs à contrainte et l'apologie que saint Augustin a faite des persécutions.* He divided his work into three parts. The first was devoted to showing that the use of force in making "conversions" destroyed the essence of Christianity. The second was given over to answering possible objections and the third to a point by point refutation of the arguments which St. Augustine had used to justify the use of force by the "true" faith.

The background of the *Commentaire philosophique,* its character as an authentic work of Protestant controversy, the Calvinist and Cartesian influence which it shows, its importance as a point of arrival for seventeenth-century Calvinism as well as a point of departure for the Enlightenment — all these have been carefully studied by Walter Rex.[3] What is important for the purpose of this present study is that the *Commentaire* represents a milestone in the development of the fideism of the *Dictionnaire,* for it was in the writing of the *Commentaire* that all of the elements of Bayle's later thought crystallized.

It was inevitable that the writing of the *Commentaire philosophique* should exercise a marked influence on the evolution of Bayle's thought. Once he had reached the conclusion that all of the arguments and commonplaces that had been hurled back and forth between the writers of the two Churches were of no avail, he had to seek new premises for his reasonings. The position to which he was pushed by the exigencies of polemics was extreme.

In order to refute the literal interpretation which Catholic writers were giving to the words "compel them to come in," Bayle abandoned all of the usual tactics of controversy. He declined to say what the parable meant, limiting himself to proving what it did *not* mean (CP, p. 367). In the *Nouvelles Lettres critiques* he had made conscience the guardian of speculative belief in the dogmas of religion. In the *Commentaire philosophique* where the question was one of morality, he made reason and the moral precepts of the Gospel and the Decalog the standards of Scriptural interpretation (*CP,* pp. 367–368). stating the principle that "la lumière naturelle, ou les principes généraux de nos connaissances sont la règle matrice et originale de toute interprétation de l'Ecriture, en matière de moeurs principalement" (*CP,* p. 367).

In so doing, Bayle was nonetheless not taking a step down the path which led to Socinianism. He was simply making use of the standard Protestant technique of establishing the principle of individual examination of the Scripture in order to forestall the possibility of any Catholic spokesman saying that the decisions of the infallible Church were not to be called into question (*CP,* pp. 369–370). And because he had earlier concluded that reason was subject to severe limitations when it undertook to examine abstract propositions he consequently qualified his rule of Scriptural interpretation to exclude the specula-tive dogmas of Christian theology, saying: "A Dieu ne plaise que je veuille étendre autant que font les sociniens la jurisdiction de la lumière naturelle et des principes métaphysiques, lorsqu'ils prétendent que tout sens donné à l'Ecriture qui n'est pas conforme à cette lumière et à ces principes-là est à rejeter et qui en vertu de cette maxime refusent de croire la Trinité et l'Incarnation" (*CP,* p. 367).

In limiting the jurisdiction of reason to the parts of Scripture which concerned the principles of morality, Bayle differed funda-mentally from the heterodox rationalists whose investigations were almost entirely in the realm of speculative knowledge. And in addi-tion, as if to put still another check on reason, he maintained that the moral precepts of the Gospel and the Decalog were its synonyms, and thus the standards of what was "right" reason, as can be seen in the following quotation: "Si en prenant [l'Ecriture] littéralement, on engage l'homme à faire des crimes (ou pour ôter toute équivoque) à commettre des actions que la lumière naturelle, les préceptes du Décalogue et la morale de l'Evangile nous défendent, il faut tenir pour tout assuré que l'on lui donne un faux sens et qu'au lieu de la révélation divine, on propose aux peuples ses visions propres, ses passions, et ses préjugés" (*CP,* p. 367). Thus, although Bayle insisted on the primacy of reason, he was in reality making the basic principles of morality the key to Scriptural interpretation.[4]

It is in this context that Bayle sets out to ruin the literal interpretation of the parable by a series of nine "proofs." The only authentically religious act, he begins, must proceed from an inner motivation. God could have no more pleasure in receiving a forced act of adoration than could a king in seeing a statue blown prostrate before him by the wind. God could not have commanded violence because violence is incapable of producing true religion (*CP,* p. 371). Violence is, moreover, contrary to the spirit of the Gospel, and because meekness, patience, and humility were the chief attributes of Jesus Christ it is a sacrilege to say that Jesus commanded violence. It is in fact this spiritual quality which makes the Gospel superior to the law of Moses (*CP,* pp. 372–373).

The third proof is that the use of violence in matters of belief would make vice indistinguishable from virtue, for every crime forbidden by the Scripture would become legitimate if done in the cause of the "true" church. There is, therefore, no crime which could not become an act of religion if the literal meaning were true (*CP,* p. 375). Bayle next profits from the contemporary Christian interest in foreign missions by saying that a commandment to use violence would furnish a plausible excuse to the infidels to bar Christian missionaries from their lands, for a king must prevent seditions, revolts, and disorders in his kingdom and would therefore have to expel all those who make vice indistinguishable from virtue (*CP,* pp. 380–381). The literal meaning would necessarily entail crimes by forcing people to act against their consciences (*CP,* p. 382). It would take away a strong argument which Christians had been using against the Mohammedans, who had spread their religion by force (*CP,* pp. 385–386). The seventh proof is that the use of violence was unknown to the earliest church fathers (*CP,* pp. 387–388), and the eighth is that the literal meaning of the parable would nullify the protests of the early Christians against the persecutions visited upon them by the pagan emperors (*CP,* p. 388).

Up to this point Bayle's arguments have been drawn from the stream of Calvinist rationalism and ethics. They contain nothing skeptical. To the contrary, one senses that the state of Bayle's confidence is high. The natural and divine revelation of morality agree.

But as closely as reason and revelation might agree in ethical questions, Bayle's next argument laid bare the gulf between reason and the theological dogmas of religion, which was the burden of his remarks on faith and reason in the *Dictionnaire*.

The ninth and last proof is that the literal meaning of the parable must be false, for it would expose the true Christians, whoever they might be, to a continuous persecution — each sect naturally believes itself to be the true church, and if Christ had desired that His word should be established by force, each sect would be itself obligated to persecute the others to compel them to come into the "true" faith. This last argument is forceful, but it was fraught with consequence since it presupposed the invincibility of error. Its significance becomes more and more evident as Bayle sets out in his scholastic fashion to pursue his adversaries into their last possible retreats.

The first objections which he imagines are not insuperable. If one objects that violence is being used only to awaken those who refuse to examine the truth, Bayle points out that the violence, in fact, has not stopped even after a person has read and meditated on Catholic arguments unless he has come into the Roman Church. And when can one tell when a man is being firm in his convictions and when he is just being stubborn? What is self-evident for one is not self-evident for another (*CP*, p. 396). If we say that God's ways are not man's ways and that violence is perhaps one of the ways God uses to bring to pass his inscrutable designs, we only throw all human and divine knowledge into doubt (*CP*, p. 397). There are, moreover, numerous examples in the Scripture to show that God has acted among men according to the way of men (*CP*, pp. 399–400).

Next comes an even stronger objection, which is that one cannot condemn the literal meaning of the parable without condemning the laws of God among the Jews, which made idolatry a capital crime, and the conduct of Moses and of Elijah, who slew the false priests of Baal. Here Bayle recognizes that he is hard pressed, and the defender of tolerance must hedge a little bit, but he answers by stating that the situations are not similar. The government of the Jews was a theocracy, God himself being its head, and idolatry could therefore be justly punished as sedition (*CP*, p. 408). Exception must likewise be made for the prophets of the Old Testament, who were acting under direct inspiration (*CP*, p. 409).

Would not his principles lead to an absurd general tolerance? Again Bayle must hedge, and he makes his defense of tolerance less than general. He excepts, specifically, tolerance of beliefs that would disturb the public peace and cause civil crimes. It would therefore be permissible not to tolerate the Roman Church, because it teaches that it must subject all the others to it when it becomes the strongest (*CP,* pp. 410–412). With this exception, he proposes a general tolerance and denies that it would have any harmful effect. If each religion were tolerated equally and did not try to force its way on the others, the result would be only a harmonious symphony of different notes, each religion vying in good works with the others (*CP,* pp. 419–422).

But the last objection is the most troublesome of all, since it comes back to the ninth proof of the first part and turns upon the invincibility of error. One might say that persecution is not in itself legitimate, but it becomes so when used in the interests of the true faith. In other words, constraint may be used in favor of the truth but not in favor of error. This question is perhaps the most important in the *Commentaire* for the development of Bayle's thought, for it caused him to continue his re-assessment of the basis of faith and reiterate the doctrine of the "erring conscience." The conscience of the heretic must be allowed all the rights of the orthodox conscience because speculative truths, which include all of the dogmas of Christianity, are not susceptible of proof, and error may be invincible. He stated categorically that ". . . il est impossible dans l'état où nous nous trouvons de connaître certainement que la vérité qui nous paraît (je parle des vérités particulières de la religion, et non pas des propriétés des nombres, ou des premiers principes de métaphysique, ou des démonstrations de géometrie) est la vérité absolue" (*CP,* p. 437).

It is impossible to attain certainty, he continued, because there is no universal and infallible mark of truth to be found either in rational evidence, which was lacking in all systems; or in incomprehensibility, for many incomprehensible things were obviously false; or in zeal, courage, and satisfaction of one's conscience, for these marks are found in every sect. Not even the Scripture, he continued, whether interpreted by the authority of the Church or by the light of individual examination, can ever lead to an idea to which no objection may be raised or maintained, for it is impossible to know whether or not any specific passage of Scripture today conveys the same meaning that its author intended (*CP,* pp. 438–439).

The invincibility of error was likewise the theme of the entire *Supplément du "Commentaire philosophique"* (1687). Feeling that the last possible objection that might be raised against his arguments for tolerance in the *Commentaire philosophique* was that one day God would punish the persecutors of orthodoxy but reward those who had persecuted heresy, Bayle set out to demonstrate that any commandment given by Christ to persecute heretics would permit heretics to lay waste the orthodox church without being guilty before God. To prove this proposition he stated that invincible error was innocent before God and that heresy was an invincible error. A judge, he maintained, who is fully persuaded of a defendant's guilt after examining the facts of the case as carefully as possible is fully justified in hanging the man even though he is really innocent. Likewise, if he is persuaded that a defendant is a heretic, the judge would be guiltless before God in punishing him, if God had commanded the use of force, although the man were in reality orthodox, for it is as difficult to define heresy as it is to determine guilt in people accused of murder (*SCP,* p. 493).

It cannot be objected, Bayle continued, that erroneous judgment in matters of religious belief comes as a result of sin — Adam made a wrong decision while he was still perfectly innocent. The real sources of error are the union of body and soul, the latter depending almost entirely on the former for the impressions which reach the brain; education, which fills us full of any number of falsities before we reach the age of reason; language, which makes it impossible for one person to make known infallibly the true intention of his thought; and the nature of questions to be examined in determining heresy (*SCP,* pp. 493–494).

Bayle dwelt at length on the last question, suggesting that God by a special grace had prevented missionaries of all churches from going to China because the various proofs which they would present against each other would destroy all confidence that the Chinese might have in Christianity. The Protestants could prove the Catholic stand wrong on Transubstantiation because it is against all of their principles of reason and metaphysics, but when they were defending the doctrines of the Trinity or the Incarnation against a Socinian they would make reason bow to faith and try to show that these doctrines, though incomprehensible, derived clearly from the Word of God. The Protestants could maintain against the Catholics that the Scripture was an adequate guide, but if someone else affirmed that Scripture alone could produce faith in a well-intentioned heart, then the Protestants would have to shift again and say that grace is necessary. The Catholics, for Bayle, were vulnerable to the same kind of objections. They could uphold their claim to authority by their antiquity, but would be put to rout by the same argument in the hands of a pagan.

And even the Scripture was not clear for, as Bayle pointed out, in all the churches there are many scholars who are not agreed on the meaning of passages of Scripture or traditions (*SCP,* pp. 494–

503). One could scarcely find three professors of the same faith agreed on the interpretation of Scripture. "De là sont venues," stated Bayle, "tant de différentes explications des mêmes passages de l'Ecriture, tant de différentes conciliations des passages qui semblent se contredire. . . . Dans les controverses chaque parti a de son côté des passages de l'Ecriture et des pères, des témoignages des plus célèbres universités, des raisons, des objections, des distinctions, des solutions, n'y ayant point de livre fait par quelque secte, auquel la secte opposée ne réponde" (*SCP,* p. 523). Bayle therefore concluded that religious controversies were difficult not only because of the prejudices and limitations of the participants, but also because of the impenetrable nature of the questions under examination, and error was consequently invincible (*SCP,* p. 503).

Although Bayle asserted in the foregoing passages that there was no certain mark of truth, he neither assumed nor advocated the skeptical attitude of indifference or suspension of judgment as some critics have held.[5] To the contrary, he shrank here, as he had done in the *Nouvelles Lettres critiques,* from the prospect of Pyrrhonism which ended in inaction (*SCP,* p. 511), and his purpose in reiterating his doctrine of the "erring conscience" was to defend Protestant liberties without coming to the impasse of skepticism (*SCP,* p. 479). He insisted that one should not suspend judgment in religious matters but should commit oneself to what seemed *nearest* to the truth, even if absolute truth were not to be found (*CP,* pp. 438, 444).

In connection with this emphasis on the authority of conscience, it should be emphasized that Bayle's belief in grace also set him apart from the skeptics, because grace, according to his idea, produced a firm persuasion in the mind. He did not believe conviction, no matter how strong, to be a rational evidence of truth, for persuasion could be produced by other factors than grace, but he maintained that even in absence of demonstrative proof, "nous croyons fermement [ce sentiment produit par la grâce], et sans le pouvoir trop soutenir à un adversaire docte et subtil, nous demeurons convaincus que c'est pourtant une vérité révélée" (*CP,* p. 439).

And as the whole first part of the *Commentaire* shows, in questions of practical morality Bayle was diametrically opposed to the skeptical position. The supposed truth ("la vérité putative") might deviate from the absolute truth in the realms of abstract knowledge, but the principles of morality, he felt, were plain: "A l'égard de la connaissance de nos devoirs pour les moeurs, la lumière révélée est si claire que peu de gens s'y trompent quand de bonne foi ils cherchent ce qui en est" (*CP,* p. 439). Lack of certainty did not trouble Bayle unduly because he believed that practical knowledge was more important than speculative knowledge, and he moreover expressed the opinion that "ni l'orthodoxie de ceux qui se trompent ni celle de ceux qui sont dans la vérité absolue n'est pas ce qui sauve; on a beau croire, si on n'est pas homme de bien, on ne sera pas sauvé" (*CP*, p. 439).

Moreover, even as hard as he had been pushed by controversy Bayle still felt in 1686 that the intellectual position of the Reformed Church was, if not ideal, at least more tenable than that of any other group. The Arminians and Socinians in founding their belief upon the authority of reason were obliged to establish every point of their doctrine with principles as evident as Descartes' *cogito,* and this, in Bayle's view, was impossible. He was likewise convinced that the Catholic position was much less defensible than the Protestant, for the former was exposed to all of the Protestant difficulties of interpretation of the Scripture (*CP*, p. 438) as well as to the overwhelming moral indictment occasioned by the use of force.

What was the state of his loyalty to the Reformed Church at this time? Devolvé maintained that in making tolerance general and in denying the Protestants the right to use civil force in questions of conscience, Bayle was "virtually the enemy of his own party."[6] The facts do not justify this view, for in setting out to convince the "persecutors" that Christ had not commanded the use of violence (*CP*, p. 430), Bayle was referring specifically to those in France who were persecuting the Huguenots.[7] In condemning examples of Protestant violence, he was not acting against the principles of his party, for he felt that no Protestant theologian would countenance the commission of crimes and violence to further the interests of the Protestant religion (*CP*, p. 365). (Bayle wrote this opinion before Jurieu openly defended the use of force by the "true" faith.) He likewise maintained that in condemning the burning of Servetus he was expressing the feeling of the vast majority of his fellow Protestants who regarded this action as "une tache hideuse des premiers temps de notre Réformation, fâcheux et déplorables restes du papisme" (*CP*, p. 415). Nor did he believe that religion in general was the cause of crimes and intolerance, for he sharply distinguished between the true spirit of religion and the abuses of it, saying:

> Mais si nous ne pouvons pas empêcher que la religion chrétienne ne demeure couverte de cette infamie [of confusing vice with virtue and of all the crimes which intolerance entails] au moins sauvons l'honneur de son fondateur et de ses lois et n'allons pas dire que tout cela s'est fait à cause qu'il nous a commandé la contrainte. Disons que les hommes n'étant pas trop accoutumés à vivre conséquemment à leurs

principes, les chrétiens n'ont pas suivi les leurs, et qu'ils ont été violents en prêchant un Evangile qui ne leur commande que la débonnaireté (*CP,* p. 380).

But the events of 1684–87 did more than reveal the gap between faith and reason. They also brought into prominence Bayle's awareness that the Reformed Church was subject to deviation and error. Both Bayle and Jurieu had answered Nicole — the philosopher in late 1684 in his *Nouvelles Lettres critiques* and the pastor in early 1686 in his *Vrai Système de l'Eglise.* In order to parry Nicole's assertion that the first Protestants could not have known whether or not they were right, both Bayle and Jurieu had stated that religious belief ultimately had to depend on subjective factors. However, Jurieu felt that Bayle had gone too far, and in another part of his *Vrai Système de l'Eglise* he criticized the doctrines of his colleague, feeling that they might lead to religious indifference.

In the meantime, Bayle had been working on his *Commentaire philosophique,* the first two parts of which appeared anonymously in late 1686. Jurieu was possibly not yet sure that Bayle was the author,[8] but in his self-appointed role of watchman on the towers of orthodoxy, he reacted violently to the "defense of the erring conscience" and general spirit of tolerance found in the *Commentaire philosophique.* He consequently attacked this new work by writing in early 1687 his *Droits des deux souverains* in which he assailed the doctrine of tolerance and advocated the use of civil authority for the establishing and defense of the "true" (Protestant) faith.

It cannot be doubted that Jurieu's attack on the rights of conscience weakened Bayle's party loyalty (which had never been overweening or fanatical). As we have seen previously, Bayle had always believed morality to be the criterium of the true Church, since, to him, one of the chief justifications for the Reformation had been the moral reform of the Church. He moreover considered the constraint put on conscience as the worst sort of immorality. Therefore, in seeing Jurieu and his followers advocating such constraint, Bayle was led to wonder whether or not God had rejected the Christians as He had the Jews and whether the Arminians and Socinians, who were heretical with regard to speculative doctrine but orthodox with regard to moral principles, were not worth at least as much as the doctrinally orthodox who had fallen into moral heresy (*SCP,* p. 535).

Bayle did not, however, push these ideas to their logical conclusion and did not abandon his belief in the Reformed Church. He rejected the idea that Jurieu's views on tolerance were the orthodox doctrine, and when the fiery pastor later insisted on them, Bayle was only the more confirmed in his belief that Jurieu was more heretical than any of the heterodox sects.

Further evidence that Bayle remained fundamentally loyal to the interests of the Reformed Church is found in his answer to Jurieu in the *Supplément du "Commentaire philosophique."* When Jurieu in his *Vrai Système de l'Eglise* and his *Droits des deux souverains* attacked Bayle's writings on conscience and tolerance, Bayle faced the alternatives of remaining silent and approving Jurieu's doctrines by default or else of engaging in an intra-Protestant dispute. However, Bayle refused to do either, and managed to escape through the horns of the dilemma. Although Jurieu had published his two above-mentioned works anonymously, giving them off as productions by two different authors, Bayle knew that Jurieu had written both of them. In one part of his *Vrai Système,* as has been mentioned, Jurieu had set forth principles which favored Bayle's stand in the *Commentaire philosophique.* Bayle therefore said simply that his views paralleled those of the "very orthodox" author of the *Vrai Système,* who contradicted and refuted the "inexperienced and unorthodox" author of the *Droits des deux souverains* (*SCP,* p. 479). In so doing, Bayle avoided a general counterattack which would have compromised the unity of the Reformed Church.

Bayle had also originally intended to devote a section of the *Supplément du "Commentaire philosophique"* to expounding "demonstrative arguments in favor of tolerance" which were to be based on the uncertainty of knowledge. He had said in the Preface of this work that he had indeed written down these arguments but that he had declined to publish them, stating:

> Ce que j'ai dit dans la troisième partie concernant la dispute que nous avons avec l'Eglise romaine touchant l'analyse de la foi, m'a fait peur à moi-même quand je l'ai considéré tout d'une suite, car j'ai montré que l'accusation de témérité que l'auteur des *Prétendus Réformés convaincus de schisme* [Nicole] a tant poussée, et en général toutes les difficultés de l'examen qui nous ont été objectées de tout temps, n'ont jamais été bien répondues que par la voie de rétorsion et de communication de ces mêmes armes aux infidèles contre le christianisme (*SCP,* p. 479).

If Bayle could refuse to promulgate arguments which he felt would work against the best interests of his church and of religion as a whole, even when such arguments would support his plea for tolerance, it is evident that he was still a loyal believer.

In summary, it was during the period 1684–1687 that Bayle took part in what he called the "grands combats de la foi et de la raison." Previous to 1684, the principles of faith (which he had acquired during his childhood, his reconversion to Protestantism, and his early training in Geneva) had coexisted more or less peacefully with the principles of reason (which he had acquired from the Protestant doctrine of individual examination, from his training in dialectics at Toulouse, and his study of Descartes in Geneva). His journalistic activities gave him the role of "historian" of the religious-rational controversy fanned by the Catholic persecution of the Huguenots. His native Protestant loyalties drew him into the dispute as a participant, and his exacting standards of dialectics precluded his using any but the most certain arguments. These factors combined to precipitate in Bayle the crisis of faith and reason, for they caused him to conclude that there is no certain mark of truth in the speculative questions of which theology is composed. He did not, however, emerge from this crisis either as an atheist or as a skeptic. His confidence in the powers of reason to deal with the philosophic ultimates had already been seriously weakened by his own "critique of pure reason," and consequently he did not feel intellectually obligated to reject the dogmas of religion simply because they did not square with the demands of rational truth. Instead of acceding to skepticism, he professed to retain his belief in the dogmas of orthodox Christianity because of the subjective factors of conscience and grace, and the course of his actions strongly indicates that, although his party loyalty was somewhat weakened by Jurieu's advocacy of intolerance, he did in fact remain a sincere and believing Protestant.

But it was the end of the line for controversy when faith and reason could no longer compete on the same grounds. In 1687 Bayle's health broke, and he had to give up his teaching and his writing of the *Nouvelles de la République des Lettres*. For over a year he was inactive in both reading and writing, and when he did recover he did not return to controversy. "C'est une chose étrange et dégoûtante que la controverse," he had said, "on n'en voit jamais la fin."[9]

NOTES

1. For examples of such books, see *NRL,* November 1686, pp. 688–690, and December 1686, p. 721.
2. *FTC, OD,* II, 350.
3. Rex, *Essays,* pp. 121–193.
4. See the comment of Serrurier, *Pierre Bayle en Hollande,* pp. 94–95.
5. See Lenient, *Etude sur Bayle,* p. 22; Cazes, *Pierre Bayle,* p. 37; Dubois, *Bayle et la tolérance,* p. 48.

6. Delvolvé, *Essai,* p. 83.

7. *CP,* p. 357. See also *SCP,* p. 479.

8. See Des Maizeaux, "Life of Bayle," p. xxxvi. But see the surmise of Rex, "Pierre Bayle: The Theology and Politics of the Article on David," *Bibliothèque d'Humanisme et Renaissance,* XXIV (1962), 186.

9. *NRL.* December, 1684, p. 193.

9 Bayle and Jurieu

ALL the elements of Bayle's views on faith and reason as they were to appear in the *Dictionnaire* had taken definite form by 1687, but in the manner of their expression between 1687 and 1697 there is the difference of night and day. The reluctance Bayle felt earlier to publish anything detrimental to the cause of the Reform was replaced in the *Dictionnaire* by a vigorous determination to state as many objections as possible to Christian belief, a circumstance which made it hard for Bayle's eighteenth-century readers to take his fideism seriously. During this ten-year period Bayle's thought underwent a basic re-orientation. Previously, it had been the inter-confessional Protestant-Catholic controversies which had so influenced the course of his thought. Now an intra-confessional dispute with his former friend and colleague Pierre Jurieu was to bring about a total change of perspective in him. During the period 1682–1687 he remained objective and lucid to the implications of what he was writing, but from 1690 on, his personal involvement blinded him to almost every other consideration.

The *Dictionnaire* period started peacefully enough. When he recuperated from his illness in 1688, he turned his attention toward matters of erudition in much the same manner as he had done during his early years before the persecution in France had called forth his abilities as a controversialist, and it was in this frame of mind that he began his *Dictionnaire* in 1689. It appears certain that the furthest thing from Bayle's mind at this time was a philosophic crusade, for he stated in one of his letters that he had undertaken to write his *Dictionnaire* only as a means of taking up his time,[1] and in a letter to his cousin de Naudis he stated that he had originally intended for his dictionary to be only a collection and correction of errors made by other writers,[2] principally Moréri in his *Grand Dictionnaire* (then in its sixth edition).

The nature of the information which Bayle was soliciting from his correspondents during 1690–1691 also testifies that his intentions at this time were without doubt irenic. Was the Joannes Serranus who translated Plato at Lausanne the same person as the historian de Serres?[3] Were certain writings of Junius Brutus attributed to Theodore de Bèze by persons who were living during Bèze's lifetime?[4] What were the values of certain ancient weights and measures? From which direction was the coldest wind in southwestern France? In gathering this information, Bayle explained, he was making "quelques recueils pour un ouvrage dont je ne sais pas encore trop bien la forme."[5]

A manuscript which, along with some of Bayle's correspondence, is now in the Royal Library of Copenhagen furnishes further evidence that when Bayle began his *Dictionnaire,* he did not contemplate the philosophic and polemic articles which accounted for most of his influence during the eighteenth century. This manuscript, bearing the date October 27, 1689, is the embryo of the *Dictionnaire.* Significantly, it contains nothing on David, the Bible, the Manicheans, the Paulicians, or the Pyrrhonians. It was studied by Emile Gigas in 1896 and again by Leif Nedergaard in 1956. Both concluded that the *Dictionnaire,* at its inception, was nothing more than a work of erudition. According to Nedergaard "ces notes reflètent uniquement l'érudition de l'historien et du philologue classique qui, d'une plume un peu pédante corrige les fautes de son prédécesseur." The judgment of Gigas was similar: " . . . cette ébauche se présente sous un aspect très pacifique et ne fait pas soupçonner les éclairs du *Dictionnaire critique,* —le grand sceptique n'est ici qu'érudit, rien de plus."[6]

Circumstances, however, were to modify the form and nature of the *Dictionnaire.* In May, 1692, Bayle published his *Projet d'un dictionnaire critique* which contained samples of his intended articles. The reaction of his friends was unfavorable, and they were able to convince Bayle that the public in general would not be interested in a book devoted solely to errors. He consequently changed the form of his work in order to appeal to the taste of the public, making the *Dictionnaire* both historical and critical and including occasional philosophic articles.[7]

But the event which had by far the greatest influence on the form and content of the *Dictionnaire* was a violent attack which Jurieu made on Bayle in 1690. This attack marked the beginning of a new period in the development and expression of Bayle's thought, for it engaged him in a bitter and irreconcilable controversy with Jurieu and his followers, removed his previous reluctance to write against a fellow Protestant, and colored his judgment to the point that he carried his personal and doctrinal counter-attack into the *Dictionnaire*.

It was the eighteenth century which fixed the image of Jurieu most often found in critical works — rash, intemperate, fanatical, and odious. Although these traits may appear in his later writings (after 1690), he was in 1674 one of the rising figures of the French Reform, a professor of theology at the Protestant Academy of Sedan, brilliant and imaginative in his defense of the Huguenots, a stirring and persuasive orator. Both by birth and by marriage he was associated with the DuMoulin family which counted so heavily in the conservative wing of French Calvinism.

At this same time, Bayle, twenty-seven, penniless, and unknown, was stagnating in the subaltern position of tutor to a provincial French family at Rouen. When the chair of history and philosophy became vacant at Sedan in 1675, it was due largely to Jurieu's backing that Bayle was the successful candidate. (Jurieu also had the ulterior motive of strengthening his own faction in the town.) When the illustrious figure extended him his protection, Bayle could not help falling under his spell.[8]

The letters which Bayle wrote to his family in southern France during this period show an attachment to Jurieu which bordered on hero worship: "Je dois mettre à la tête de mes bons amis M. Jurieu and toute sa maison . . . C'est un des premiers hommes de ce siècle sans contredit . . .[9] And although Bayle had been under the influence of the liberal and tolerant tradition of the *école de Saumur*[10] while he was a student at Geneva, he was now under the ascendency of the more rigid and conservative Jurieu, combatting Jurieu's enemies and condemning on hearsay evidence the moderately liberal tendencies of Pajon, his sense of fairness being momentarily in eclipse.[11] After the Protestant Academy of Sedan was dissolved in 1681, Bayle planned to go to Normandy ". . . où M. Jurieu était appelé" to wait for help from his friends, but when the offer came from Rotterdam, he decided to go there instead " . . . considérant que M. Jurieu s'y en allait aussi . . . "[12]

Upon their arrival in Holland as refugees, Bayle still continued to admire Jurieu. He praised his books[13] and considered it no small compliment that his own *Critique générale* (which had appeared anonymously in 1682) had been attributed to Jurieu.[14] He considered Jurieu the champion of the Protestant cause[15] and heartily approved his vehement point by point refutation of Maimbourg's *Histoire du calvinisme*.[16] Jurieu, for his part, seemed well disposed to all of

Bayle's family and had even offered to help Bayle's younger brother, Joseph, find a position in Holland.[17]

Once in Rotterdam, however, the philosopher and the pastor started to grow apart socially and intellectually. Their work habits were different, and they saw each other only infrequently.[18] In addition, Bayle started to discern in Jurieu evidences of a haughty and rash temperament and to realize how easily he took offense.[19] He also became somewhat critical of Jurieu's methods of controversy, disapproving of the bitterness *(aigreur)* in the latter's *Esprit de M. Arnaud* as well as of his use of falsified information in the same work.[20] But more important, the *"patron-client"* relationship was beginning to change. Bayle was winning a reputation as an author that threatened to eclipse Jurieu's own, and the pastor reacted dourly to that turn of events.[21]

The cleavage between the two men became more pronounced around 1686. Jurieu began to look askance at some of Bayle's doctrines, and Bayle in turn concluded that some of Jurieu's doctrines were contradictory and morally unsound. Jurieu had examined Bayle's doctrine of the "erring conscience" and Bayle's arguments for tolerance as they had appeared in the *Nouvelles Lettres critiques* in 1684. When Jurieu wrote his *Vrai Système de l'Eglise* in February 1686, he criticized Bayle's doctrine of the "erring conscience," which held that error sincerely believed should be accorded all the privileges of truth. But at the same time, in another part of his same work, Jurieu maintained essentially the same doctrine, stating that even if the first Reformers had been wrong in their belief, they would have been morally obligated to break away from the Catholic Church because they believed in their consciences that they were right.[22] Bayle affirmed more vigorously than ever in the *Commentaire philosophique* (late 1686) that no temporal power had the right to constrain conscience. Jurieu answered directly with his *Droits des deux souverains* (1687), insisting vehemently on the right of the temporal powers to suppress heresy.

To Bayle, the appeal to force was a flagrant contradiction with the position that Jurieu had taken in his *Vrai Système de l'Eglise.* From various references in the Preface to the *Supplément du "Commentaire philosophique"* (1687), which was Bayle's answer to the *Droits des deux souverains,* it becomes evident that Bayle now considered Jurieu presumptuous to assign himself the role of sentinel and spokesman for the true faith without being more consistent in his doctrines.[23] Moreover, in attacking the *Commentaire philosophique,* said Bayle, Jurieu had not even understood the question and had "pursued a fantom" because of his habit of reading superficially and judging hastily. To Bayle, who was always very scrupulous in attempting to understand his opponent's point of view, this procedure was criminal negligence, and he upbraided his ostensibly anonymous opponent, saying: "En effet, les lecteurs habiles ne pardonnent jamais à quiconque examine si négligemment ce qu'il réfute qu'il ose attribuer à son adversaire, et le réfuter sur ce pied-là, le contraire de ce qu'il a enseigné."[24] In another connection, when he was commenting on the *Droits des deux souverains,* Bayle stated: "L'auteur de ce traité paraît fort bon Protestant, ce qui est de plus fâcheux; car il donnera lieu de penser que nous sommes encore dans les sentiments des premiers réformateurs touchant la peine des hérétiques, ce qui énerverait et affadirait la plupart des plaintes que nous publions contre la France."[25] Bayle felt that Jurieu's rashness and temerity were doing the Protestant cause more harm than good.

Another circumstance which further separated the two was the publication in 1686 of a book by Jurieu entitled *L'Accomplissement des prophéties ou la déliverance prochaine de l'Eglise* which purported to be the true interpretation of the Apocalypse of St. John. In it Jurieu proclaimed that the Papacy, which he believed to be the reign of the Antichrist, would fall in 1689, at which time the Reformed Church would be restored to power in France by royal authority. He further predicted that France would be converted to Protestantism, which would then reign for a thousand years.

Bayle had long since come to believe that the Apocalypse of St. John was a potential reef for all Bible commentators. He likewise believed that explanations of St. John's vision were liable to be extravagant and fanatic.[26] (In holding this belief, Bayle was again following in the tradition of Calvin, who had refused to attempt an interpretation of the Apocalypse.) One may therefore be permitted to conjecture that Bayle lost much of his confidence in Jurieu when the latter published his *Accomplissements des prophéties* in 1686, for Jurieu claimed therein to have discovered hidden meanings in the Apocalypse which all previous scriptorians had failed to see. Bayle gave Jurieu's book a very impartial review in the *Nouvelles de la République des Lettres,* but he added that "... les esprits philosophiques n'y mordront pas avec toute la sensibilité que [ces matières] méritent."[27]

But in spite of these important differences of temperament and point of view, there was as yet no open break between the two. Bayle remained in agreement with many of Jurieu's teachings. The latter had set forth the idea of a more or less universal church in one part of his *Vrai Système* and had affirmed that crime was more serious than error, both of which ideas Bayle accepted.[28] Bayle gives no indication of any serious personal animosity existing between the two of them at the time. They were still on good terms in July 1688.[29] Bayle continued to visit him occasionally[30] and continued to think of him as a friend, writing to Minutoli that ". . . il a été dangereusement malade, mais Dieu l'a rendu à nos prières. . . ."[31]

When 1689, the date announced by Jurieu for the deliverance of the Church, had come and gone with no change in the political scene, Jurieu announced the doctrine that the restoration of the refugees would take place by force, that William of Orange had been raised up especially for that task, and that subjects had the right to break their contract with their sovereign whenever the latter was unjust. This was tantamount to calling upon the Huguenots still in France to revolt.

Two anonymous pamphlets appeared in reaction to the inflammatory tone of Jurieu's teachings: *La Réponse d'un nouveau converti à la lettre d'un réfugié* (1689) and *Avis important aux réfugiés sur leur prochain retour en France* (April 1690). The essence of the first was that until the Protestants disowned any advocacy of intolerance, the violence which they had suffered in France was fully justified. The pamphlet's particular objects of attack were Jurieu's pastoral letters and extravagant interpretations of the Apocalypse and the spirit of sedition and rebellion which emanated from them. The second pamphlet developed the same theme more fully and dwelt especially on the satiric and seditious pamphlets, gazettes, and *feuilles volantes* which originated among the refugees and which were directed against France.

About this same time Bayle received from his Swiss friend Minutoli a *Projet de paix* which had been devised by a certain merchant in Geneva named Goudet. The latter had asked Minutoli to make several copies of his project and to send them to Holland, there to be shown to various influential people in order to have their opinion. Bayle agreed to do Minutoli this favor and consequently had a number of copies made. One of them inadvertently fell into the hands of Jurieu, who now linked Bayle with a monstrous conspiracy which had its head in the court of France and which had as its intention the undoing of the Allies and the Reformed Church.[32]

From Jurieu's point of view (in retrospect in 1691) Bayle had earlier given way to the "libertinage de son coeur et de son imagination" ever since the publication of the *Pensées diverses sur la comète* in 1682. Bayle's *Critique générale* of the Jesuit Maimbourg had shown "un coeur entièrement gâté," and after the *Commentaire philo-*

sophique, Jurieu saw that "le mal était sans remède." When he came to believe that Bayle was the author of the *Avis aux réfugiés,* he said that "j'en eus horreur, ce qui me fit concevoir le personnage comme l'un des plus méchants hommes du monde." [33]

Jurieu had just started to denounce his colleague as the author of the *Avis* when he discovered the *Projet de paix.* He then appended to his *Examen d'un libelle contre la religion, contre l'état, et contre la révolution d'Angleterre, intitulé "Avis important aux réfugiés sur leur prochain retour en France"* an "Avis important au Public" in which he denounced Bayle as an impious and profane person, an atheist, a traitor and deceiver, an enemy to the state deserving of capital punishment.

A letter of March, 1691, to Minutoli shows that resentment and indignation had been building up with Bayle: ". . . je ne vous cèlerai plus les justes sujets de ressentiment que j'ai contre M. Jurieu, et sur quoi j'aurais eu toujours une extrême retenue, s'il n'eût le premier voulu rompre." [34] When Bayle did finally answer, all of the resentment which he had been harboring exploded. He was so indignant at what he felt were the treacherous and temerarious procedures employed by Jurieu that in the *Cabale chimérique* (May 1691), which was the first reply he made to Jurieu's public accusations, he angrily abandoned the reserve and moderation he had maintained until that time, saying:

> [Les amis de M. Jurieu] auront grand tort s'ils se plaignent que je ne garde pas la modération qui m'est si naturelle, comme le savent tous ceux dont je suis connu. J'ai un déplaisir inconcevable de me voir forcé à sortir de mon état naturel par la plus cruelle et la plus sanglante injure que l'on puisse faire à un homme d'honneur. Tout ce qui se peut dire de plus atroce et de plus infâme a été publié contre moi. Je ne dois donc pas être blâmé si je repousse vivement les calomnies d'un si furieux persécuteur. S'il n'avait voulu que me faire assassiner ou empoisonner, je fais assez peu de cas de la vie pour avoir été capable de me taire; mais avec la vie il a voulu me ravir l'honneur, il a voulu que je laissasse ma tête sur un échafaud comme traître, criminel de lèze-majesté, conspirateur contre la Hollande où je suis en charge publique; et il a voulu envelopper dans la même peine et dans la même infamie mes meilleurs amis, personnes d'un mérite distingué. C'est à quoi il n'y a point de patience qui soit à l'épreuve. [35]

A war of pamphlets ensued, lasting from May 1691 until August 1692. Bayle's attack on Jurieu was bitter, relentless, irreconcilable and personal. Pride, temerity, ambition, malice, and the spirit of vengeance — all of these he now saw in his former friend against whom he continuously inveighed. [36]

During this bitter dispute, Bayle took leave of his objectivity and from 1691 on, his correspondence and writings abound with personal judgments where Jurieu is concerned. When he had previously seen Jurieu criticized by various factions, he had dismissed this opposition as the lot of great men.[37] Now he mentioned similar opposition to show that Jurieu was the "mépris et l'horreur des personnes les plus éclairées."[38] Bayle felt that "tout homme de bon goût . . . jugera que jamais accusateur ne s'est embarrassé dans plus de faussetés, de contradictions, et de puérilités que le mien,"[39] and he was sure that Jurieu was universally censured by "les plus sensés."[40] In his own correspondence, he referred to Jurieu scornfully as "le prophète," "notre visionnaire," or "Orkius"[41] and he denounced him as a Tartuffe.[42]

So great was Bayle's loss of perspective that his counterattack became both personal and doctrinal, and in the *Cabale chimérique* he announced:

> J'examinerai dans ma réponse les reproches qu'il me fait d'avoir rempli mes livres de maximes dangereuses, et lui montrerai qu'à son dam et pour ses péchés il a touché à cette corde. Ah! qu'il me donne un beau champ pour faire voir que jamais auteur n'a fait de livres aussi capables que les siens de gâter le coeur et l'esprit, et d'introduire la superstition et le fanatisme, la plus opposée de toutes les pestes au culte raisonnable et à cette solide piété que Dieu rétablit dans le monde au dernier siècle par le moyen de nos glorieux réformateurs.[43]

Bayle reported on this same page that a new work with this precise intent was about ready to be published. This was his own *Janua Coelorum reserata,* in which he undertook to show that the principles laid down by Jurieu in his *Vrai Système de l'Eglise* opened the gates of Heaven to every sect in the world.[44]

When Bayle wrote his *Projet d'un dictionnaire critique* (May 1692), he asserted in connection with Moréri's Catholic bias that nothing was more ridiculous than a dictionary which indulged in controversy. Ironically, Bayle, by that time, had so much lost his own objectivity with regard to Jurieu that he brought his own personal and doctrinal quarrel with the prophet-pastor into the *Projet d'un dictionnaire critique,* and he did not hesitate to carry it from there into the *Dictionnaire* itself. When he was criticized for engaging in a personal feud in a work of erudition, Bayle answered:

> Quant aux petits coups de fouet qu'il a eus dans le *Projet du dictionnaire,* j'avoue que tous les lecteurs . . . les ont trouvés mal placés, et je ne saurais disconvenir qu'il n'eût mieux valu que cet ouvrage eût été exempt de ces petites hostilités. Contre tout autre adversaire je les aurais évitées avec soin, mais c'est un homme qui semble être d'une espèce toute particulière et qui fait exception à tout engagement d'honnêteté. Il tire avantage principalement, lui et ses créatures, de

ce qu'on ne lui répond pas vertement. Il en prend matière d'insulter; c'est pourquoi j'ai cru qu'il fallait le traiter comme à coups de fourche.[45]

It was shortly after the publication of the *Projet d'un dictionnaire critique* that the war of pamphlets ceased, and Bayle seems to have laid aside, at least temporarily, the idea of attacking Jurieu in the *Dictionnaire*. However, around December 1692, when he heard rumors that Jurieu was attempting to have him relieved of his teaching position, Bayle wrote to Gisbert Cuperus, one of his friends in the dominant Orangist party, seeking his support. Since Cuperus was also on good terms with Jurieu, there is also the distinct possibility that Bayle meant to warn the pastor by saying: ". . . j'ai dessein de séparer toute passion et toute rancune de mon dictionnaire, où d'ailleurs, si je voulais, je ferais entrer de toutes parts mon délateur, et par le pied et par la tête d'une manière qui le chagrinerait beaucoup . . ."[46]

This appeal for support was unsuccessful, for while Jurieu abandoned his accusations centered around the *Projet de Paix* and the *Avis aux réfugiés,* he complained before the Flemish Consistory that the *Pensées diverses sur la comète* contained pernicious and irreligious doctrines (the magistrates and the Walloon Consistory had refused to move from their strictly impartial position toward the two antagonists). Since most of this Consistory did not know French, Jurieu had excerpts of the book translated into Flemish, twisting Bayle's intention in so doing. At the same time, the Flemish Consistory of Rotterdam was examining a defense of a liberal Flemish minister named Balthasar Bekker who in his book *De Betooverde Wereld* denied the influence of the Devil on man. The conservative Consistory, alarmed that a minister should deny the Devil and that a prominent Protestant should "defend" atheism, issued a severe condemnation of Bayle's *Pensées diverses.*

Meanwhile, the magistrates favorable to Bayle (his original protector, Paets, had been a strong Republican) had been replaced in October 1692 by others more favorable to the Orangist party of the *stathouder* William III. Jurieu took advantage of his favor and Bayle's disfavor with the Orangists to present before the city magistrates the consistorial censure of the *Pensées diverses* and to request that Bayle's position as professor of philosophy and history at the *École illustre* be withdrawn. Jurieu's machinations were successful, and Bayle lost his post on October 30, 1693.

Even after this *coup,* Jurieu did not cease his efforts to bring about Bayle's further downfall. On December 19, 1693, he exhorted the Walloon Consistory to "avoir égard au grand scandale que souffrent plusieurs âmes chrétiennes de voir approcher le sieur Bayle de la table sacrée," and he submitted extracts from Bayle's books to be examined. Bayle countered by writing especially for the Consistory an *Addition aux Pensées diverses* (1694). The members of the Walloon Consistory were more cautious than the Flemish Consistory had been, however, and having appointed a committee to read the entire books, they continued to discuss the question for the next two years. In addition, during January and February of 1694 Jurieu preached two sermons on the theme that it was permissible to hate one's neighbor for the greater glory of God. Bayle answered the challenge in a pamphlet entitled *Nouvelle Hérésie dans la morale.* Bayle's denunciation of Jurieu's "moral heresy" was also added to the agenda of the Consistory and remained there for two years.[47] Thus, the polemics between Bayle and Jurieu were in progress the entire period during which the *Dictionnaire* was being written.

It is not surprising, therefore, to find that Bayle made good his threat to bring Jurieu into the *Dictionnaire* "et par le pied et par la tête." He had refrained from doing so before losing his post, for the first sixty pages of the *Dictionnaire* (up to the article "Accius") had been printed by November 13, 1693, and they contain no mention of Jurieu's books.[48] However, in the article "Adam (Jean)" which was printed by December 29, 1693,[49] Bayle gave his adversary another "coup de fourche" for his extravagant imaginings which had caused him to falsify the position of his opponents.[50] Thereafter Bayle seldom missed an opportunity to show the contradictions and inconsistencies in Jurieu's predictions and doctrines.

Bayle's personal and doctrinal attack on Jurieu accounts for many of the passages in the *Dictionnaire* which made this work the arsenal of the *philosophes,* but there are a number of other such "irreligious" passages which transcend the level of personalities and which are aimed at fanaticism and human pride in general. Nonetheless, these passages appear likewise to have had their origin in Bayle's quarrel with Jurieu, for in writing against Jurieu, Bayle found himself at war with a powerful faction of Jurieu's followers. Bayle had never had a fanatical party loyalty and had earlier noted a moral decline in Protestantism. Now, after his condemnation by the Flemish Consistory, he censured Protestant bad faith and ethical lapses as he had previously criticized the moral deviations which he had seen in the Catholic Church.[51]

In all of his previous works, his purpose had been to evaluate, criticize, or refute, and he had always had in mind a particular objective, whether to reveal the inconsistencies in the supposition that comets are harbingers of misfortune or to refute Maimbourg's defamation of Calvinism. Now, in the *Dictionnaire* he envisaged a somewhat larger sphere of action. One of his targets was human pride, the incarnation of which he saw in Jurieu and those who resembled him. One cannot help hearing echoes of the controversy which had been raging for eighteen months when Bayle declared in the *Projet d'un dictionnaire* that his intended dictionary of errors would not only facilitate the search for truth for those studying the fine arts and history, but would also have a moral value. Pride, he continued, is the antithesis of the true Christian spirit. Therefore, in seeing demonstrated the weakness of man's reason, the nothingness of his knowledge, and the passions which have swayed human judgment in all ages, one should become more reticent to pronounce rash or hasty judgments upon his fellow men and should come nearer to the humility required by the Gospel.[52]

Indeed, it is difficult to find any passages in the *Dictionnaire* which set forth the rational difficulties of religious dogmas without finding the desire to humble the arrogance of theologians, to silence useless dispute, or to confute Jurieu. The "anti-religious" elements of the article on the prophet Mohammed, for example, were in reality censures of the prophet Jurieu. Bayle first attacked his former colleague's doctrine of intolerance by suggesting that it reduced Christianity to the same moral level as the false religion of Islam.[53] He next argues that the Mohammedans were more Christian (tolerant) than Jurieu, for while the Gospel commanded only meekness and persuasion in winning converts, Jurieu was preaching violence and force. The Mohammedans, on the other hand, said Bayle, officially advocated the use of force to promulgate their religion, but they had lately become more tolerant in their dealings with conquered countries.[54] And finally, he claimed that the variations within the Koran were an evidence of its falsity, adding that in this the Koran resembled very strangely the modern explanations of the Apocalypse, such as Jurieu's own, which changed "selon les nouvelles de la gazette."[55] Similarly, of the nine full pages in the article "Socin (Fauste)," two and a half were devoted to an attack on Jurieu (who despised the Socinians above all else), showing that he was either a slanderer for having accused Port Royal of Socinianism, or else, by his own proofs, he was a Socinian himself.[56] And Bayle also maintained in the article "Xénophane," that Jurieu's doctrine was as pernicious as that of Spinoza.[57]

One of the articles which the *philosophes* used most devastatingly was the article "David." Yet in a brilliant and solidly-documented study, Walter Rex has shown that the supposed attack on the Bible and the prophet-king David was in reality intended as an attack on the political-prophet Jurieu, clearly understood in Bayle's milieu by his contemporaries but misinterpreted in another milieu by posterity.[58]

Significantly, the article "Pyrrhon," which contains the *Dictionnaire's* most reasoned array of philosophic skepticism seems also to be closely related to the controversy with Jurieu. In the article "Pyrrhon," Bayle's entire purpose in elaborating on the difficulties which surrounded Christian dogmas was to confute an imaginary theologian who was the archetype of self-satisfied pride.[59] And Jurieu himself was not forgotten, for Bayle in another note declared:

> [Les pyrrhoniens] ne faisaient ferme nulle part. A toute heure ils se sentaient prêts de raisonner d'une nouvelle manière, selon les variations des occurrences. Un certain docteur en théologie en fait autant [Jurieu is cited in the marginal note] . . . [Saurin] lui fait voir qu'il établit des principes selon le besoin qui le presse, et dès qu'ils commencent à l'incommoder, il en subroge de tout contraires. . . .[60]

Bayle concluded that even though Jurieu was as opinionated as Pyrrhon had been skeptical, the reasonings of the former were less valid than those of the latter.

Once Bayle had decided to enlarge the scope of the *Dictionnaire* and to include philosophical articles, it is likely that the article "Pyrrhon" would have been written in some form, for the religious controversies ten years before had revealed the depth of the epistemological problem of either rational or Christian belief. One may also conjecture that he would have treated the question of evil. The events of the past ten years had given him eloquent witness of the reality of the evil in the world to be reconciled with the idea of an omnipotent and benevolent Providence, and the long-extinct Manichean heresy offered a convenient framework within which to explore a dualistic hypothesis in contrast to the monism of Calvinism.

It is revealing of the nature of the *Dictionnaire* that the genuine philosophic content of the articles "Marcionites," "Manichéens," and "Pauliciens" — the ones dealing with evil and having the most "antireligious" reasoning — is put to an immediate and polemical use. And in none of the three articles is Jurieu ever far from sight. In the first, while there are three and a half pages of notes giving the details of a dispute between Jurieu and Maimbourg, during which Bayle takes Jurieu to task for his bad reasoning and faulty conclusions, there is only one page devoted to the doctrine of the Marcionites. In the article "Pauliciens," which is really only the continuation and conclusion of the article "Manichéens,[61] Bayle again dwelt at length on the inconsistencies of Jurieu's doctrine which changed according to the exigencies of controversy, and he said in conclusion: "Vous avez ici en petit le caractère de ce docteur: il n'y a nulle justesse dans ses censures, nulle liaison dans ses dogmes. Tout y est plein d'inconséquences; l'inégalité, les contradictions, les variations règnent dans tous ses ouvrages. Ceux qui prendraient la peine de les éplucher trouveraient à tout moment une matière de critique comme celle-ci." [62]

What is more important in the articles on the Manicheans and the Paulicians is that Bayle's real motive for setting forth the difficulties of all systems with regard to the problem of evil was, according to his own explanations, to show that no one should dispute about the dogmas of religion. Jurieu was again the particular object of this moral, for after having shown that all systems encountered unanswerable objections when they undertook to explain the origin of evil, Bayle reminded his readers that Jurieu, in his *Jugements sur les méthodes rigides et relâchées d'expliquer la grâce* (1686), had arrived at essentially the same fideistic position held by himself.

It is difficult, Jurieu had said, to understand how God could embody all perfection and goodness and at the same time be the cause of all events, including evil ones. But if this position of absolute predestination is difficult to maintain, he continued, all others are even more difficult, and he concluded by saying that if anyone could offer a more suitable solution to the question of evil, he stood ready to accept it. Bayle now takes a malicious pleasure in having a Manichean show that he, an absurd heretic, could on rational grounds explain the origin of evil better than could Jurieu, and Bayle then concludes with this important statement:

> Finissons par le bon usage à quoi je destine ces remarques. Il est plus utile qu'on ne pense d'humilier la raison de l'homme en lui montrant avec quelle force les hérésies les plus folles, comme sont celles des manichéens, se jouent de ses lumières pour embrouiller les vérités les plus capitales. . . . Que faut-il donc faire? Il faut captiver son entendement sous l'obéissance de la foi et ne disputer jamais sur certaines choses. [63]

At the end of the article Bayle reiterated in a note which he added for the second edition in 1702 that the reason for which he brought up these questions was to teach people not to dispute about them. Foreseeing that the only possible defense against a Manichean is to say that God's ways are inscrutable to man, Bayle said:

> C'est bien dit, et voilà où il fallait se fixer. C'est revenir au commencement de la lice: il aurait fallu n'en point partir; car il est inutile de s'engager à la dispute, si après avoir couru quelque temps

l'on est obligé de s'enfermer dans sa thèse . . . il vaut mieux en convenir dès le début et s'arrêter là, et laisser courir comme de vaines
chicaneries les objections des philosophes et n'y opposer que le silence
avec le bouclier de la foi.[64]

But could Bayle really have written against Jurieu as he did
without feeling that he was attacking the Reformed Church as such?
Once again the Rotterdam philosopher is easily misread if he is not
placed in his milieu. It would have been difficult, if not impossible, to
attack the doctrine of Bossuet or any Catholic bishop without attacking
the whole Catholic Church because of the doctrinal homogeneity and
ecclesiastical discipline. The Reform, on the other hand, was much
more diverse and complex, and Jurieu was not always considered by
other Protestants to be the incarnation of orthodoxy.

It is true that Jurieu frequently looked upon himself as a watchman
on the towers of orthodoxy,[65] and he also had considerable influence in
the proceedings of the synods, even though not in an official capacity.
However, the same attributes which had won Jurieu his influence
made him enemies. Some of his enemies were personal, such as those
who took offense at his doctrines, such as those at Sedan who in 1676
had been "shocked" by his doctrine concerning baptism.[67]

Jurieu's enemies were not all among the lay members, but were
as a matter of fact more frequently among the officials of the Reformed
Church. In 1670 Jurieu had been censured by the Synod of Saintonge
for his answer to the minister D'Huisseau of Saumur concerning the
reunion of the Catholic and Protestant faiths. Later, his doctrine on
baptism had been condemned by a synod as had been several propositions in his *Apologie de la Morale des Réformés*.[68] In 1686 the
Flemish synods, which were traditionally the most conservative, condemned his doctrine of the thousand-year reign described in his
Accomplissements des prophéties.[69] A censure by the Walloon Synod
of Breda in September 1692 confirmed previous doctrinal censures
by the Synods of Middelbourg, Bolduc, and Campen, and rejected
Jurieu's demand that previous synodal resolutions be altered to omit
decisions which were unfavorable to him.[70] It is also interesting to note
that Jurieu had accused another minister, Le Gendre, of heterodoxy,
but the Walloon Consistory approved the latter's doctrines.[71] Another
pastor, Ysarn, among the reputedly conservative and orthodox of
the Walloon Church, attacked Jurieu's doctrine of baptism.[72] Finally,
Jurieu found himself at odds with Saurin, one of the most eminent of
the refugee ministers, who roundly took him to task at the Synod of
Ziric-Zee in May 1692, and who later published a full-scale critique
of Jurieu's doctrines.[73]

In view of the Protestant opposition to Jurieu's doctrines and tactics one must necessarily conclude that Bayle could easily have attacked Jurieu's theological and ethical principles and at the same time believed his own to be sound and orthodox. His writings and correspondence show that such was precisely his attitude. He had come to believe that Jurieu, in his doctrines and conduct, overturned the morality of the Gospel, and hence he was not to be considered a representative of or spokesman for the Reformed Church:

> Le Saint Esprit n'a pas tellement abandonné l'Eglise réformée de France dans sa dispersion, qu'il n'y soit demeuré de bonnes âmes qui sont encore persuadées malgré les déclamations et les livres de M. Jurieu qu'il faut aimer ceux qui nous haissent, prier pour ceux qui nous persécutent, souffrir patiemment pour le nom de Dieu, ne rendre point le mal pour le mal, l'injure pour l'injure, ni écrire des satires. Que les ennemis de notre sainte Réformation soient donc avertis ici par mon moyen que c'est une calomnie atroce d'un enfant ingrat et dénaturé contre l'Eglise qui lui a donné naissance que d'accuser, comme il fait, de n'être pas bons protestants, mais plutôt des personnes sans religion, ceux qui recommandent la morale de l'évangile.[74]

Elsewhere is found much evidence to indicate that during the period 1691–1697 the tenets and spirit of Calvinism continued to be the basis of Bayle's thought. It would be imagined, for example, that if he were the militant opponent of all belief in the supernatural, he would have been in full sympathy with the Flemish minister Balthasar Bekker who denied the influence of the Devil. Although the Flemish Consistory considered both Bayle and Bekker to be of the same cloth, Bayle indicated that he by no means shared Bekker's ideas. Writing to friends in Switzerland he said "Vous avez ouï parler, sans doute, d'un ministre d'Amsterdam, nommé Bekker, qui a publié en flamand un gros livre pour prouver qu'il n'y a point de diables qui aient aucun pouvoir sur la terre. Les synodes ont justement pris l'alarme de cela; l'affaire fait grand bruit; les magistrats d'Amsterdam en doivent prendre connaissance. Plusieurs, dit-on, ont donné dans les rêveries de cet homme."[75] The French translation of Bekker's work did not appear until 1693, but the fact that Bayle rejected and termed "rêverie" the idea that anyone could deny the power of the Devil shows that he still retained this basic orthodox idea.

It is noteworthy also that Bayle invariably stated the conviction that he was orthodox and declared himself ready, for example, to show that "mes *Comètes* ne contiennent rien qui soit contraire ou à la droite raison ou à l'Ecriture, ou à la Confession de foi des Eglises réformées."[76] And his ideas on tolerance did not stem from religious indifference, for he wrote that the Reformed minister Huet, upon being

attacked by Jurieu, had answered that he favored only political tolerance, ". . . laissant les sociniens pour ce qu'ils sont et se gardant bien
de se donner la peine de voir si on outre ou non leurs sentiments. Cette
déclaration m'a bien plu, car autrement on donnerait lieu de croire
que ceux qui écrivent pour la tolérance ne jugent pas que les erreurs
pour lesquelles ils la demandent soient grièves: pensée qui peut
convenir aux partisans de la *tolérance ecclésiastique;* mais non de la
tolérance politique, qui n'est qu'une exemption des lois pénales."[77]

He always identified himself with the Protestant cause and
deplored the ministerial divisions, which he believed to be caused
entirely by Jurieu.[78] It is also revealing that when a Paris bookseller
wanted to import a number of copies of the *Dictionnaire* into France,
Bayle stated dryly that "M. le chancelier . . . donnerait [la permission]
pourvu que le livre ne contînt rien contre l'Etat ni contre la religion
catholique. Jugez si ces conditions se peuvent trouver dans l'ouvrage
d'un protestant qui est en Hollande."[79]

NOTES

1. Letter to Silvestre, 19 Sept. 92, *OD,* IV, 679.

2. Letter to his cousin De Naudis, 22 May 92, *LFam, OD,* I, 161.

3. Letter to Constant 16/26 July 90, *OD,* IV, 644.

4. Letter to Minutoli, 3 Dec. 91, *OD,* IV, 669.

5. Letter to his cousin De Naudis, 3 Dec. 91, *LFam, OD,* I, 159.

6. Gigas, "Première Ebauche d'un ouvrage célèbre," *Bulletin de la Commis-sion de l'histoire des églises wallonnes,* 2nd series, Vol. II (1896), pp. 66–68, and Nedergaard, "La Genèse du 'Dictionnaire historique et critique' de Pierre Bayle," *Orbis Litterarum,* XIII (1958), 214.

7. *DHC,* I, i-ii. See also letter to Silvestre, 19 Sept. 92, *OD,* IV, 679.

8. Labrousse, *Pierre Bayle,* I, 131–132.

9. Letter to his father, 29 Jan. 76, *LFam, OD,* I, 64. See also letter to his older brother, 16 Dec. 76, *LFam, OD,* I, p. 73. See also Richard Popkin, "An Unpublished Letter of Pierre Bayle to Pierre Jurieu," in *Pierre Bayle, le philosophe de Rotterdam,* p. 218.

10. Walter Rex, "Pierre Bayle, Louis Tronchin et la querelle des donatistes: Etude d'un document inédit," *BSHPF* (Juillet-Septembre, 1959), pp. 104–105.

11. Labrousse, *Pierre Bayle,* I, 155–157.

12. Letter to his father, 8 Dec. 81, *LFam, OD,* I, 129.

13. Letter to Rou, no date, 1684, *OD,* IV, 612.

14. Letter to his younger brother, 3 Oct. 82, *LFam, OD,* I, 135.

15. See *NRL,* April 1685, *OD,* I, 260.

16. See *OD,* II, 338.

17. Letter from Bayle to his younger brother, 16 June 82, *LFam, OD,* I, 132.

18. Letter from Bayle to his younger brother, 10 April 84, *LFam, OD*, I, 147.

19. Letter to his younger brother, 10 April 84, *LFam, OD*, I, 145.

20. Letter to Lenfant, 8 March 84, *OD, IV*, 613. See also the letter to his brother 9 Jan. 84, *NL*, II, 213–214.

21. Labrousse, *Pierre Bayle*, I, 193–196, gives a detailed account of this changing relationship.

22. Walter Rex, in his *Essays on Pierre Bayle and Religious Controversy* (The Hague, 1964), pp. 145–152, gives an excellent treatment of Jurieu's intellectual development as it was affected by the Protestant-Catholic controversies over the Church and the Eucharist.

23. *SCP, OD*, II, 478.

24. Letter to the publisher which Bayle had inserted at the beginning of the third volume of the *Commentaire philosophique, OD*, II, 444.

25. *SCP, OD*, II, 478.

26. See *PDC, OD*, III, 155–156.

27. *NRL*, September 1686, *OD*, I, 643.

28. *NRL*, April 1686, *OD*, I, 525–526.

29. Letter to Lenfant, 20 July 88, *OD*, IV, 635.

30. Letter to Rou, 27 Feb. 89, *OD*, IV, 638.

31. 6 Oct. 89, *OD*, IV, 641.

32. Des Maizeaux, "Life of Bayle," pp. xxxix-xl.

33. Pierre Jurieu, *Apologie du Sr. Jurieu, Pasteur et professeur en théologie, adressée aux pasteurs et conducteurs des églises wallonnes des Pays-Bas* (La Haye, 1691), p. 24.

34. 26 March 91, *OD*, IV, 657.

35. *CC, OD*, II, 631.

36. Quotations on this subject are almost superfluous, examples being found on nearly every page of the pamphlets which Bayle wrote against Jurieu. See especially the *Cabale chimérique, OD*, II, 702, 709, 719, 744; *Entretiens sur le grand scandale causé par un livre intitulé: La Cabale chimérique, OD*, II, 679–680.

37. See letter from Bayle to his father, 4 Oct. 76, *LFam, OD*, I, 71, and the letter to his older brother, 26 March 82, *LFam, OD*, I, 131.

38. Letter to his cousin de Bruguières, 24 Dec. 91, *LFam, OD*, I, 160.

39. Letter to Constant, 18 Feb. 92, *OD*, IV, 673.

40. Letter to Minutoli, 26 March 91, *OD*, IV, 657.

41. Cf. letter to Constant, 8 Oct. 91, *OD*, IV, 667.

42. Letter to his cousin De Naudis 24 Dec. 91, *NL*, II, 289. See also *OD*, II, 712, where Bayle cited a pasage from Molière's *Le Tartuffe* and applied it to Jurieu.

43. *CC, OD*, II, 642.

44. In the *Dictionnaire* Bayle stated that he had chosen the title *Janua Coelorum reserata* because of its similarity with *Janua Linguarum reserata*, a famous book by Comenius, who like Jurieu had pronounced a number of rash and unfulfilled prophecies based on the Apocalypse. After commenting that his own work (*Janua Coelorum reserata*) completely refuted Jurieu's *Vrai Système de l'Eglise*, Bayle revealed his reason for writing against his former colleague: "Ceci est fâcheux pour M. Jurieu; car c'est lui arracher la meilleure plume de l'aile, c'est ruiner l'ouvrage qui lui faisait le plus d'honneur." *DHC*, "Comenius," note N, I, 914.

45. Letter to Silvestre, 19 Sept. 92, *OD*, IV, 679.

46. 1 Dec. 92, ed. J. L. Gerig and G. L. van Roosbroek, "Unpublished Letters of Pierre Bayle," *Romanic Review,* XXIII (1932), 22.

47. Hazewinkel, "Pierre Bayle à Rotterdam," in *Pierre Bayle, le philosophe de Rotterdam,* pp. 33–40.

48. See letter to Du Rondel, 13 Nov. 93, *OD,* IV, 704.

49. See letter to Du Rondel, 29 Dec. 93, *OD,* IV, 706.

50. *DHC,* "Adam (Jean)," note E, 1st ed. (1697), I, 100.

51. Letter to his cousin, 28 Dec. 93, *LFam, OD,* I, 170. Also letter to Sylvestre, 17 Dec. 91, *OD,* IV, 671.

52. *Projet d'un dictionnaire, DHC,* IV, 2983-2984. See also Des Maizeaux, "Life of Bayle," p. lxxvi.

53. *DHC,* "Mahomet," note O, III, 1854–1855.

54. "Mahomet," note AA, pp. 1859–1860.

55. "Mahomet," note NN, p. 1865.

56. *DHC,* "Socin (Fauste)," notes M and N, III, 2612–2614.

57. "Xénophane," note L, IV, 2896. Other instances of Bayle's attacks on Jurieu are found in the articles "Tavernier," note E, IV, 2697–2698; "Nicole," note D, III, 2089–2090; "Augustin," note H, I, 392; "Luther," note R, III, 1822; "Eséchiel," note C, II, 1110; "Marests," note D, III, 1914–1915; "Zeurius Boxhornius," note P, IV, 2933–2938.

58. Walter Rex, "The Theology and Politics of the Article of David," *Bibliothèque d'humanisme et de Renaissance,* XXIV (1962), 168–189, and XXV (1963), 366–403.

59. See "Pyrrhon," note B, III, 2306–2308.

60. "Pyrrhon," note F, p. 2309.

61. See "Pauliciens," note E, III, 2201.

62. "Pauliciens," note I, pp. 2211–2212.

63. "Pauliciens," note F, pp. 2206–2208.

64. "Pauliciens," note M, p. 2214.

65. See *SCP, OD,* II, 478; also *OD,* IV, 644, note.

66. Frank Paux, *Les Précurseurs français de la Tolérance au xvlle siècle* (Paris, 1880), p. 126. The background of all such controversies is treated by Erich Haase, *Einführung in die Literatur des Refuge: Der Beitrag der französischen Protestanten zur Entwicklung analytischer Denkformen am Ende des 17. Jahrhunderts* (Berlin, 1959).

67. Letter from Bayle to his father, 4 Oct. 76, *LFam, OD,* I, 71.

68. Des Maizeaux, "Life of Bayle," pp. ix-x, note.

69. *OD,* IV, 635, note.

70. Letter from Bayle to Minutoli, 6 Oct. 92, *OD,* IV, 680.

71. Letter from Bayle to Constant, 8 Oct. 91, *OD,* IV, 667.

72. See letter from Bayle to Constant, 29 Nov. 94 *OD,* IV, 713.

73. *OD,* IV, 713, note.

74. *CC, OD,* II, 625. See also letter to Rou, 18 May 91, *OD,* IV, 659, and letter to De Bruguières, 22 May 92, *LFam, OD,* I, 160.

75. 3 Dec. 91, *OD,* IV, 669. See also letter to Constant, 18 Feb. 92, *OD,* IV, 673.

76. Letter to his cousin, 28 Dec. 93, *NL,* II, 335–336, 338. See also letter to Du Rondel, 13 Nov. 93, *OD,* IV, 704.

77. Letter to Constant, 16/26 July 90, *OD,* IV, 645.

78. Letter to De Bruguières, 11 Aug. 92, *LFam, OD,* I, 163.

79. Letter to his cousin, 8 March 97, *LFam, OD,* I, 180.

10   Bayle and the Censors

BEFORE passing to conclusions and a summary of Bayle's attitudes toward faith and reason, there remains one more major question to treat, that of his sincerity. That he was somehow among the believers is the only position tenable if his expressions in the *Dictionnaire* are authentic. It is for this reason that those critics who have placed Bayle outside the religious context have had to assume that he was forced by the power of the state or the Church to adopt a veneer of orthodoxy in order to get his books published or in order to avoid fine or imprisonment. A variation of this view is that Bayle did not disguise his "real" thought but instead put it in the notes of his *Dictionnaire* in order to elude the censor. These familiar assertions are contradicted, however, by two facts: (1) that the liberty prevailing in Bayle's Dutch milieu was so extensive that it precluded the necessity of any dissimulation or falsification on his part, and (2) that Bayle's acts and temperament give convincing evidence that he expressed his views on faith and reason freely and without any fear of civil or ecclesiastical authorities.

Much confusion concerning Bayle's supposed insincerity and subterfuges has resulted from the failure to remember that Bayle wrote and published all of his works in the Republic of Holland and not in France. When Bayle was driven from France in 1681, the French government was completely centralized, and the French Church and State together exercised a strict and preventive censorship over all that was printed. Under these conditions the Encyclopedists of the mid-eighteenth century necessarily had recourse to all sorts of ruses in order to print and disseminate their works. When Bayle arrived in Rotterdam in 1681, however, he found an entirely different atmosphere than prevailed in the realm of the Sun King, for the Republic of Holland at that time was nothing more than a loose confederation of seven independent states. These states were loyally united in time of war, but in time of peace they were divided by jealousies and, on occasion, open hostilities. Each city had its own laws and was related to the rest of the country only through the Assembly of the States General to which it sent its representatives.[1] The States General made decisions about laws and taxes which were in general only "des exhortations ou des conseils, dont les grandes villes se permettaient de discuter l'opportunité."[2]

Moreover, toleration was an official policy of the Dutch states. The governing class was composed mainly of aristocrats who belonged to the liberal Remonstrant (Arminian) party and who consequently accepted the principle of religious toleration as an integral part of their belief.[3] There was, however, an even more cogent reason than religious precept which led the Dutch rulers to establish and maintain religious toleration — the Dutch economy depended on trade, trade depended on civil peace, and civil peace in turn depended on toleration of conflicting creeds.[4] Besides, being surrounded by powerful neighbors, the Dutch felt themselves obliged to respect the religious practices of foreign diplomats in Holland. Thus, even though only the Reformed Church was officially sanctioned, Catholics and others enjoyed a practical toleration.[5] In describing Dutch tolerance, Bayle reported in his review, *Les Nouvelles de la République des Lettres,* that Catholics could come and go as they wished and that they had twenty-six chapels and more priests to celebrate the Mass than the Protestants had ministers to preach.[6]

It is not surprising, then, to learn that in Bayle's Dutch milieu there existed a freedom of the press that was for all practical purposes complete. The Dutch States attempted to control only those writings which threatened foreign relations or civil peace, and even in so doing, they did not institute a preventive censorship.[7] It is true that the States of Holland granted a license, or *privilège,* to certain books, but the Dutch did not follow the French practice of using the license as a means of controlling thought. The Dutch license was simply a form of copyright which gave the publisher the exclusive right to print or sell a specified book during a limited length of time, ordinarily five, ten, fifteen, or twenty years. The license was not necessary in order to publish, and in granting it, the Dutch States did not require a censor to examine the book for subversive or heretical teachings. In fact, they specifically declared that they neither approved nor disapproved the contents of the book in question.[8]

It has become a commonplace that Bayle used the system of notes in the *Dictionnaire,* as one eminent literary historian recently put it, in order "to hide away in these closely-printed notes amid the learned references his dangerous thoughts and queries, hoping that the censor would nod his head wearily and approve by default what otherwise was sure to be forbidden."[9] One of the most certain things about Bayle and his *Dictionnaire,* however, is that he neither modified nor dissimulated the expression of his thought for the purpose of deceiving the governmental censor and thus obtaining the permission to publish. Such a censor was non-existent, and the obtaining of a license (which in any event was not necessary in order to publish) did not depend upon the orthodoxy of the views expressed by the author.

Could Bayle conceivably have used his system of notes in order to deceive the French censor and thus get the *Dictionnaire* approved in France? This supposition does not seem admissible, for Bayle wanted the work banned in France, in order to protect the interests of his Dutch publisher. It was the design of certain printers in Lyons to pirate his work, and if anything, Bayle seemed bent on thwarting their design by insuring its interdiction.[10]

In reality, the only source of pressure upon any theological writer was the conservative wing of the Dutch and French Reformed churches. Many Reformed ministers were of a liberal temperament, especially among the French refugees, but there were others who willingly would have used strict measures to prevent the printing or distribution of heterodox books. Although these ministers held no civil authority, they could petition the local city magistrates or the States General to ban offensive books. The civil powers occasionally granted such petitions for various reasons and issued decrees forbidding the further publication or sale of the books in question.

The influence of the Reformed clergy, however, was not great enough to justify the assumption that Bayle's protests of orthodoxy were forced or insincere. In any event, it is altogether improbable that they were inspired by fear of fine or imprisonment. Willem Knuttel, in a study of all books banned in the Republic of Holland, points out that since governmental controls were almost invariably aimed at the printer and bookseller, the author of a condemned book ran no personal danger unless the book had political overtones. Knuttel was able to find titles of only twelve theological works banned during the twenty-six years that Bayle was in Holland, and he reports that no civil action of any kind was taken against any of the authors.[11] The attitude of the Dutch States toward Spinoza is significant, for this despised philosopher was considered the most impious and heterodox writer in Holland, and yet Siccama points out that "[il] n'eut d'autres persécutions à subir dans sa personne que celle de la synagogue juive."[12]

CARL A. RUDISILL LIBRARY
LENOIR RHYNE COLLEGE

Indeed, the Reformed Church failed conspicuously in its occasional attempts to exercise control over the press, for the Dutch civil authorities, in addition to being inclined to toleration generally, were slow and ineffective when they decided for some expedience to ban a book. In the first place, they would take no action against a book until some complaint had been brought against it, by which time it would have been in circulation for months or even years. One book published in 1685 was condemned as late as 1740 because it had then become a center of controversy.[13] Likewise, the edition of the book in question might have been completely sold by the time any official decision had been reached. Previous reference has been made to Bekker's book entitled *Der Betooverde Wereld* (The Enchanted World) in which he attacked several common beliefs concerning miracles and the devil. The Dutch synods, feeling that the book was dangerous, had managed to have it banned in Utrecht and for four years had petitioned the States General to condemn it throughout the Republic. But the States did not look with favor upon this petition, and they finally decided that so many copies of the book had been sold during their deliberations that banning it would not help the situation. Knuttel states that there were many similar examples.[14]

Moreover, because there was no central authority in Holland, it was rare that a book would be condemned by the States General. (Knuttel reports that books so banned formed only a very small minority of the ones discovered by his study.)[15] Since jurisdiction over booksellers and printers was normally confined to the local city authorities,[16] it was not unusual for a book to be banned in one state but to be on sale in the others,[17] as was the case with Bekker's *Betooverde Wereld,* which circulated freely in six of the states of Holland, although it had been banned in Utrecht.[18]

It should also be pointed out that most of the decrees against objectionable books had been issued in consequence of outside pressure or influence and were consequently not enforced with any rigor. One *feuille volante,* for instance, was suppressed in the French version but reprinted three times in Dutch without any repercussions.[19] Hobbes' *Leviathan* had been published in English in Amsterdam in 1667. Some seven years later, after the Peace of Westminster, the Court of England brought enough pressure to bear on the Dutch States to have the edition banned. This condemnation of the work did not, however, prevent the publication of a Dutch translation in 1678.[20] It is true that whenever a foreign power protested through its ambassador, the magistrates of the city concerned issued a decree against the publisher in question or sometimes a general warning to all printers and booksellers, but the decree was not ordinarily enforced rigorously, and it would fall into disuse until there were more protests.[21]

The Dutch magistrates were generally equally unenthusiastic about enforcing bannings which had been obtained through the influence of the Reformed clergy, for more often than not, there was friction between the civil and the ecclesiastical authorities. The condemning of theological books did not at all reflect official disapproval, and the magistrates often went through the formalities of banning a book only in order to end the "perpetual pestering" by the Flemish synods.[22] Siccama also reports that synodal petitions resulted in the banning of a number of theological works, but at the same time he points out that "ces interdictions étaient vaines bien souvent, et l'Etat se refusait à prendre des mesures plus efficaces pour protéger la pureté de la foi contre les théories des philosophes."[23] And not infrequently, the civil authorities simply refused to acquiesce in the demands of the synods, as has been pointed out in the case of Bekker's *Betooverde Wereld*.[24]

The influence of the Reformed Church over the press was also seriously curtailed by divisions within the Church itself. Various synods, for example, had enjoined the Reformed ministers not to publish any theological writings without first submitting them to examination by the appropriate consistorial committee, but the majority of the ministers in Holland did not abide by this decision.[25] In fact, the French Reformed Church in Holland was so beset with tensions and divisions during Bayle's sojourn there that it could not even act with authority on its own internal affairs, much less present a united front to the civil authorities.[26] In France the influence of the Catholic Church over the French press was keenly felt because the Church was unified and was acting in concert with an authoritarian government. In Holland, both the Reformed Church and the States of Holland were split into numerous factions which were very often working at cross purposes with each other, and any effort by the Dutch and French Protestants to control the expression of thought was doomed to failure.

It seems evident, then, that if Bayle had really desired to attack the orthodox faith, he could easily have done so directly, as had the Pajonist minister Le Cène. After having been expelled from the Reformed Church in 1686 for his liberal ideas concerning grace, Le Cène did not hesitate to declare "une guerre sans merci aux anciennes doctrines, et allant droit au but, il signalait toutes les inconséquences de la dogmatique réformée."[27] Even though Le Cène was openly and vigorously attacking the established Reformed Church, his books were not banned, and no action was taken against him by the civil government.

But possibly the most convincing evidence that Bayle did not fear the decrees of the civil government is found in his conduct during his dispute with Pierre Jurieu. After Bayle first answered the impetuous pastor in his *Cabale chimérique* (1691), Jurieu requested the magistrates to prohibit Bayle from writing any more against him. Jurieu must have been chagrined to hear the magistrates prohibit either of the two antagonists from writing against the other. Almost immediately, Jurieu disregarded this prohibition and proceeded to bring forth several violent pamphlets against his former friend. Bayle also defied the decree of the city authorities, and the war of pamphlets was resumed without any attempt by the magistrates to enforce their injunction.[28]

Bayle also showed by concrete acts that he refused to be swayed by the influence of the Rotterdam Consistory when he did not believe its decisions to be just. In 1697, just after the publication of the *Dictionnaire,* Jurieu's followers became predominant in the Consistory for the first time, and at Jurieu's instigation they had a committee examine the articles "David," "Pyrrhon," "Manichéens," and "Pauliciens." Bayle showed himself to be very conciliatory, and he promised that for the second edition of his *Dictionnaire* he would write explanations of the objectionable parts of the philosophic articles and would rewrite the article on David.

His avowed object in doing so was to avoid a public controversy which would not be edifying to the Church, but he refused to change his doctrine on faith and reason, except to make it more emphatic, declaring that if the Consistory did not find his proposals acceptable, he would not shrink from entering into such polemics.[29]

It is also apparent that Bayle could not have feared losing personal and social advantages by openly stating his thought, for one of his most striking characteristics was his independence and his lack of worldly ambition. In 1684 he had written to his younger brother:

> De la manière dont Dieu m'a fait, c'est mon élément qu'un état de médiocrité. Le grand jour m'incommode, j'aime l'obscurité et un état médiocre et tranquille. ... Ainsi qu'on ne me blâme point de ce je croupis à Rotterdam, et même qu'on ne me plaigne pas, car ce qu'un autre regarderait comme une prison et comme un anéantissement indigne, je le trouve si conforme à mon humeur que je ne le changerais pas pour une condition brillante.[30]

He was still of the same persuasion in 1693, after having lost his post at the *École illustre*. In writing to Minutoli he confided:

> J'ai reçu ma disgrâce comme doit faire un philosophe chrétien, et je continue, Dieu merci, à posséder mon âme dans une grande tranquillité. La douceur et le repos dans les études où je me suis engagé et où je me plais, seront cause que je me tiendrai dans cette ville, si on m'y laisse, pour le moins jusqu'à ce que mon *Dictionnaire* soit achevé d'imprimer. . . . Du reste, n'étant ni amateur du bien, ni des honneurs, je me soucierai peu d'avoir des vocations, et je n'en accepterais pas quand bien même on m'en adresserait. Je n'aime point assez les conflits, les cabales, et les entremangeries professorales qui règnent dans toutes nos académies. *Canam mihi et musis.*[31]

If Bayle was intimidated by neither the civil nor the Church authorities, and he was not swayed by personal interest, the only remaining objection which one might raise concerning his sincerity is the possibility that he intended for the whole fabric of his writings to be ironical and that, as Lévy-Bruhl has suggested, in deploring the "weakness and helplessness of reason," he really meant to point out the "absurdity of revelation."[32]

It is true that in the sense of "derisive invective" or occasionally "blame by praise," shafts of irony are strewn through the works of Bayle. And in his guise as a Catholic author in the *Pensées diverses* and as a "learned Presbyterian" in the *Commentaire philosophique* there is an irony of dissimulation. But these asides and initial poses are of a completely secondary importance. Whoever has followed Bayle through hundreds of *in-folio* pages cannot help seeing that his intent is to establish a proposition as a hard and solid fact. The essence of his method was to make his arguments so clear and demonstrative that no objection could be raised against them, which is diametrically opposed to the Voltarian practice of affirming by denying and denying by affirming. Additional insight into Bayle's approach to controversial questions is given by an unpublished letter of 1674 in which he showed a distinct aversion to the types of "oblique attack" which Voltaire was to perfect and to employ so masterfully. The Jesuit Father Maimbroug in his *Histoire de l'arianisme* had attacked the Jansenists of Port Royal while ostensibly writing against the Arian heretics. Bayle disapproved of this procedure, saying that it had not had "tout le bon effet qu'il en attendait peut-être, car ces voies obliques, ces attaques clandestines ont je ne sais quoi de choquant même pour ceux qui observent la neutralité entre les jésuites et les jansénistes."[33]

Bayle was in fact so different from the Encyclopedists and Voltaire in his way of thinking that he often failed even to perceive the subtleties of raillery, persiflage, and irony, much less to use them as his chief means of attack, as some critics have assumed he did. An excellent example of Bayle's unexpected naïveté is found in his reaction to a letter which Fontenelle sent him in 1686 to be inserted in the *Nouvelles de la République des Lettres*. The letter was supposedly written by an explorer recently returned from Borneo, and in a manner worthy of Voltaire it described the wars which two queens, Mreo and her daughter Eenegu, had been waging against each other. According to the latest rumors, the letter reported, the troops of Mreo, although composed completely of eunuchs, had surprised their adversaries and had obliged them to swear allegiance to Mreo. Bayle, seeing neither an obvious allusion to the recent Revocation of the Edict of Nantes nor even the meaning of the transparent anagrams, believed ingenuously that the letter spoke only of actual events taking place in Borneo. Twenty years later, he confessed in a letter to Des Maizeaux that neither he nor Jurieu had suspected the double meaning of the letter.[34] It seems clear from this revealing example that Bayle was manifestly not of the temperament to make irony the basis of his supposed attack on Christian theology.

In summary, nothing in Bayle's actions and milieu justifies the supposition that his position concerning faith and reason in the *Dictionnaire* is not the authentic expression of his real views. He obviously did not try to hide his true thought from the censor in order to have his works printed because no preventive censorship was ever exercised by the States of Holland. No civil body cared what he wrote, and he did not fear the Reformed Church, which in any case was powerless to control the expression of thought. His lack of worldly and pecuniary ambition precluded any material interest that he might have had in dissimulating what he really thought. At the same time, his temperament and use of irony were at the opposite pole from the Voltairian irony sometimes attributed to him. Until evidence can be submitted to the contrary, his sincerity must remain unimpugned.

NOTES

1. Jacques Siccama, "A tous les coeurs bien nés, que la patrie est chère," in *La Hollande et la liberté de penser* (Paris, 1884), pp. 106–107.
2. Eugène Hatin, *Les Gazettes de Hollande et la presse clandestine aux XVIIe et XVIIIe siècles* (Paris, 1865), p. 93.
3. Cornelia Serrurier, *Pierre Bayle en Hollande,* pp. 30–31.
4. R. Murris, *La Hollande et les Hollandais au XVIIe et au XVIIIe siècles vus par les Français* (Paris, 1925), p. 226.
5. G. Cohen, "Le Séjour de Saint-Evremond en Hollande," RLC, V (1925), 442.

6. March, 1685, in Bayle's *Oeuvres diverses,* I (La Haye, 1737), 249.

7. Siccama, "A tous les coeurs," pp. 110–111.

8. This limitation of time distinguished the license from another form of copyright, the *jus copiae,* which gave the right of ownership to the work and which could be willed or transmitted by cession. See Charles Pieters, *Annales de l'imprimerie des Elsevier, ou histoire de leur famille et de leurs éditions* (Gand, 1858), p. xxix. See also *DHC,* IV, 3010, where Bayle explains the nature of the *privilège.*

9. George R. Havens, *The Age of Ideas* (New York, 1955), p. 34.

10. Letter to Janiçon, 21 March 1697, "Lettres inédites de Pierre Bayle," *RHL,* ed. Paul Denis, XIX (1912), 925. But why did Bayle use the system of notes and text if not to deceive or lull the censor? The reason is easily found in his other works and correspondence where one sees his propensity for digression and erudition. The extensive use of notes was simply Bayle's way of being able to report all that he knew on a given subject without being cramped by the exigencies of style and coherence.

11. Knuttel, *Verboden Boeken in de Republiek der Vereeingde Nederlanden* ('s-Gravenhage, 1914), pp. vii, xi.

12. Siccama, "A tous les coeurs," p. 152.

13. Knuttel, *Verboden Boeken,* p. vii.

14. Knuttel, *Verboden Boeken,* pp. x–xi.

15. Knuttel, *Verboden Boeken,* p. xi.

16. See *Lettres, mémoires et négociations du comte d'Estrades* (La Haye, 1719), IV, 225, cited in Hatin, *Gazettes,* p. 92, for an example of the difficulties which the French ambassador encountered in attempting to prevent a Dutch printer from publishing libels against the French throne.

17. Siccama, "A tous les coeurs," pp. 111–112.

18. Knuttel, *Verboden Boeken,* p. x.

19. Knuttel, *Verboden Boeken,* p. ix.

20. Siccama, "A tous les coeurs," p. 128–129.

21. For examples, see Hatin, *Gazettes,* p. 89, and Siccama, "A tous les coeurs," pp. 131–132.

22. Knuttel, *Verboden Boeken,* p. xi.

23. Siccama, "A tous les coeurs," p. 151.

24. Knuttel, *Verboden Boeken,* p. x. Bayle gives another example of the real antagonism existing between the civil and the ecclesiastical authorities in a letter to Constant, January 1691, in *Oeuvres diverses,* IV, 652.

25. Frank Puaux, *Les Précurseurs français de la tolérance au XVIIe siècle* (Paris, 1880), p. 118.

26. R. Mirandolle, "A propos d'une lettre de Pierre Jurieu," *Bulletin de la Commission de l'histoire des églises wallonnes,* 2nd series, II (1898), 244.

27. Puaux, *Les Précurseurs,* p. 110.

28. Hazewinkel, "Pierre Bayle à Rotterdam," in *Pierre Bayle, le philosophe de Rotterdam,* p. 33.

29. J. Kan, "Bayle et Jurieu," *Bulletin de la Commission de l'histoire des églises wallonnes,* 1st series, IV (1889), 185–199.

30. 10 April 1684, in *Oeuvres diverses,* I, 146.

31. 8 March, 1694, in *Oeuvres diverses,* IV, 707–708.

32. Lévy-Bruhl, "Pierre Bayle," *Open Court,* xii (1898), 662.

33. Letter to Minutoli, 12 July 74, Leyden University MS, Marchandi Codex No. 4.

34. Elizabeth Labrousse, "Les Coulisses du journal de Bayle," in *Pierre Bayle, le philosophe de Rotterdam,* pp. 111–112.

Conclusions

AFTER following Bayle on the long and sometimes devious path which led to the *Dictionnaire,* we must come back to the questions posed at the beginning of this study. Was the expression of fideism in the *Dictionnaire* genuine? The answer must be "Yes." It was the position he came to naturally as the heterogenous elements of his early years — a critical mode of thought derived from Calvinist and Cartesian rationalism, a sense of the corruptness of the world, a feeling of the deep workings of grace, and the strong Calvinist emphasis on the ethical life — were worked upon by the stresses and pressures of religious controversy and philosophic preoccupation with the problem of evil. There was, moreover, no apparent and substantial motive for him to dissimulate. In some way, he must be classed among the believers.

Was he an orthodox believer in the Reformed Church? Here the way is a little more hedged up. If thousands of ponderous theological volumes have not been able to prove conclusively who holds the original faith, it would be indiscreet to try to settle the question here. It should be sufficient to say that the overwhelming weight of facts indicates that Bayle at least thought himself to be an orthodox believer.

This view, of course, runs directly counter to what is still the popular image of Bayle — the skeptic, the consciously unorthodox antagonist, the spiritual *frondeur,* the religious fifth columnist. But this latter image, it must be remembered, was formed by the *philosophes,* who simply found it incredible that one who spent his life reasoning could be serious in speaking of the debility of reason. And Bayle was close enough to the *philosophes* on a number of points — tolerance, rejection of superstition, anti-clericalism, and the disparity between reason and Christian theology — that they felt he must have been speaking outside any orthodoxy (an image, incidentally, which Bayle's contemporary enemies had helped to create).

The *philosophes* likewise failed to see that each of the points of resemblance which Bayle bore to them was a part of a long religious tradition. Calvinists had been taking a hard look at superstitions for over 150 years. Bayle's plea for tolerance in the *Commentaire philosophique* was based on essentially religious premises, and his polemical tactics were modeled on those of his Calvinist contemporaries and predecessors. The eighteenth-century deists gave more emphasis to ethics than to theology, as did Bayle, but such, paradoxically, had also been the tendency of much of seventeenth-century Calvinism, although in a different way and to a different degree. When Bayle occasionally became anti-clerical, the burden of his criticism was directed toward those clerics who, in his opinion, had abandoned the moral tradition of the Gospel. He attacked Calvinists, but not Calvinism; religionists, but not religion, and this distinction is capital. The idea that there is a great gulf between human reason and divine faith was as old in Christianity as St. Paul's first letter to the Corinthians, and it had not always ended in irreligion.

It is not difficult to see why the *philosophes* could so easily misunderstand this Protestant refugee. Their background was entirely different from his, and they saw him and the subjects he wrote about through the eyes of their generation and not his. Having no deep cultural commitment to religious faith, and being imbued with a spirit of rationalism, they naturally assumed that the author of the *Dictionnaire* shared their views. It must be admitted, too, that Bayle's rigorous, intense, and exhaustive style was not one calculated to "plaire aux cavaliers et aux dames," to use his own description of it, and it often obscured his real intention for anyone who did not follow him through long pages of syllogistic reasoning.

The *philosophes* were right enough about one aspect of Bayle's doctrine of faith — as it was expressed in the *Dictionnaire* it was not at all conducive to faith, and one might justly question the intentions of one who attempts to edify the faithful by proposing long lists of the difficulties which attend belief in Christian dogmas. But here again Bayle's intention must be sought in his milieu.

Though his views on faith and reason developed naturally and authentically, their expression in the *Dictionnaire* was more than a carefully-considered statement of belief. Bayle's purpose was also polemic and personal. They were so many shafts aimed the most frequently at specific targets within a rather limited milieu, at Jurieu in particular, and because of his bitter fight with Jurieu, at theological arrogance in general. If in the manner of Voltaire Bayle had signed his letters with a motto, it might well have been "confound the presumptuous," which is still a long way from "écrasez l'infâme." But there is little to justify the idea that Bayle's intentions anywhere include such a general crusade as undertaken by Voltaire. He lacked the confidence in human nature which always undergirds the zeal of the reformer. His work and objectives were always more personal and his targets were immediate.

If the critique of Christian faith in the *Dictionnaire* was destructive of religious belief, which it was, the disservice to faith must still be charged largely to the account of the faithful. Its origin is to be found in the mutual attacks of the believers, which laid bare the vulnerable chinks in the armor of each of them, and in the intolerance which did much to discredit organized religion. It is here that the study of Bayle's thought and influence throws a somewhat different light on the transition period between the seventeenth and eighteenth centuries. Instead of seeing religious belief gradually succumbing to ever-increasing assaults from the outside, one sees that the most destructive forces came from within.

Bayle's importance historically is due to what he wrote on faith and reason, to the way in which his ideas were understood and transformed by his intellectual successors. But to understand the man himself, one must probe deeper into his religion. And for this, it is not enough to say that Bayle considered himself an orthodox believer and to show that his doctrinal stance was in the Calvinist tradition. Religion must be more than ideas. As William James pointed out, creeds, whether personal or confessional, are only the codification of the religious attitude and experience. The measure of religion must therefore include assessment of attitudes as well as the analysis of ideas. It must include consideration of the successive states of one's confidence as well as one's doctrinal resting places. Bayle's religion can best be described in terms of his changing attitudes toward the objects around which his religious life centered — Providence, the Reform, and the moral life.

His early correspondence (until about 1685) reveals a consummate confidence in the workings of Providence, which he felt was guiding, protecting and upholding the elect, or the "little flock." His concomitant belief in the reality of Grace during this period is also easily discernible, the Grace which calls and persuades, which frees the heart from the dominion of the passions and turns it to the righteous life. At the same time the new Cartesian rationalism with its critical approach provided both a counterbalance to religious enthusiasm and a solid buttress to his early faith. The experience at Geneva under the influence of the *école de Saumur* built in him the confidence that reason is a kind of moral revelation which complements the Scripture in the defense of the Calvinist doctrines. Bayle's religion of this early period may be characterized by confidence in the ordering of the world, commitment to the moral life, and absence of basic doubts and hesitations. If he at one time was uncertain which confession, the Catholic or the Protestant, was right, he had no doubts that one of them was right, and his return to Protestantism after his eighteen-month conversion to Catholicism only served to strengthen his conviction that the divine truth was to be found in the Reformed Church.

His confidence in the intellectual position of the Reform suffered some little attrition during the period 1682–87 when he figured prominently in Protestant-Catholic polemics. The Cartesian rationalism which he had seen at Geneva as a bulwark of Protestant faith became hostile and destructive in the hands of a Catholic, such as Nicole, and even more so in the hands of a libertine or deist. At the same time, the textual criticism of Father Simon led Bayle to preclude the Scripture as infallible authority although he still retained a subjective belief in it. These two conclusions, big with implication, still did not destroy his confidence in the Reform and its doctrines, for even if the polemics in which he was engaged showed that no system was completely defensible, he still believed that Calvinism was the most defensible. It was also during this period that he made a sweeping reassessment of the powers of reason and concluded that the human intellect was incapable of dealing with ultimate philosophical questions. Yet he still believed very strongly in the moral life, which was in his view the essence of religion. It is perhaps in Part I of the *Commentaire philosophique* that we find the high-water mark of his faith, a virile confidence in reason as a moral guide even though its powers in speculative questions were severely limited.

Bayle had previously felt that there had been a moral decline in Protestantism, and his faith in the Reform was shaken quite severely during 1686–87 by the intolerance and fanaticism of some of his fellow Protestants and even more after his long quarrel with Jurieu began in 1690. Bayle remained within the Reformed Church by taking the position that his adversaries were morally heretical. But during his later life it is very difficult to find the same solid confidence in the Reform as in his early years.

It appears to be in his same period (from 1685 on) that the fact of evil in the world obscured Bayle's idea of and attitudes toward

Providence. As early as 1682, in the *Pensées diverses,* Bayle's mind was occupied occasionally with the question of evil, but the revocation of the Edict of Nantes in 1685 and the attendant plight of the elect, whom Bayle expected should in some way enjoy the protection of God, made the question of evil real. The triumph of injustice was further accentuated by the fact that Bayle's brother, Jacob, died during the persecution of the Huguenots in 1685. From this point on, Bayle's attitude toward Providence changed from one of confidence and expectation to one of resignation. During this period, as during his early years, there is a conspicuous lack of the existential *angoisse* of a Pascal, but even though the belief in a divine ordering of events might be present, God's relations with the world had become inscrutable. Bayle's attitude toward Providence at this time seems to have been essentially passive, a kind of spiritual dead end.

For religion is perhaps in its essence a dialogue between man and God, in which what is most genuinely human reaches out for and responds to what it perceives as the Divine. In order for a faith to be vivifying, God and man must be on speaking terms. Man must perceive, or feel that he perceives the Divine at work in the world. In this sense the faith in Providence proposed in the *Dictionnaire* was not vivifying. It was an act of submission, an avowal that God's workings were not recognizable in the world. Even though it was the point to which Bayle kept returning after long rational sallies and explorations had proved unfruitful, the fideistic attitude in this sense represented a defeat.

But what Bayle had always considered the voice of God to man in the most direct way was conscience, charting the path of the ethical life even if only a step ahead, and this confidence he maintained throughout his life. One might object that the Stoic resignation and detachment and the emphasis on ethics are simply the position of the deist, but in that case one would have to count the Old Testament prophet Micah among the deists when he said that the whole duty of men was "to love mercy, do justly, and to walk humbly before thy God." (Micah 6:8) Bayle's moral concepts were likewise religiously oriented, and they were the response that he made to what he perceived as the Divine.

To be sure, this accent is not the only one to be found in all of Bayle's writings after the *Dictionnaire (Réponse aux questions d'un provincial,* 1703; *Continuation des "Pensées diverses,"* 1704; *Entretiens de Maxime et de Thémiste,* 1706). During the last four years of his life, he was engaged almost constantly in polemics. His opponents were, not surprisingly, liberal rationalists, such as Jacques Bernard,

Isaac Jacquelot, and Jean Le Clerc, with whom Jurieu now allied himself, and a tone of personal animosity sometimes entered in. It is this personal virulence which more than anything else would give evidence of the occasional loss of the religious attitude, but this tone is not omnipresent in Bayle's works and did not permeate his whole being. In the sense of the Calvinist moral life, Bayle remained religious to a great degree to the end.

And one might conjecture that in another sense within the definition given, Bayle's religious background continued to manifest itself. He never ceased to grapple with the questions involving man and God, and when he died on December 28, 1706, it was only after having furnished copy to the printer for his latest work on the uses of faith and reason. It is not inconceivable that the greatest fruit, if not evidence, of Bayle's religious life, spent at the crossroads of faith and reason, was that until the very end, he kept up his part of the dialogue.

Bibliography

Adam, Antoine. *Histoire de la littérature française au XVIIe siècle.* 5 vols. Paris, 1956.

André, Paul. *La Jeunesse de Bayle, tribun de la tolérance.* Geneva, 1953.

Andrieu, Jules. *La Censure et la police des livres en France sous l'ancien régime.* Agen, 1884.

Ascoli, Georges. "Bayle et l'Avis aux réfugiés," *Revue d'histoire littéraire,* XX (1913), 517–545.

——. "Deux pamphlets inédits de Pierre Bayle contre le maréchal de Luxembourg (1680)," *Revue des livres anciens,* II (1914–1917), 76–109.

Atkinson, Geoffroy. "Précurseurs de Bayle et de Fontenelle (la comète de 1664–1665 et *l'Incrèdulité savante*)," *Révue de littérature comparée,* XXV (1951), 12–42.

Barber, W. H. *Leibniz in France from Arnauld to Voltaire.* New York, 1955.

——. "Pierre Bayle: Faith and Reason," In *The French Mind: Studies in Honour of Gustave Rudler,* ed. Will Moore. Oxford, 1952.

Barnes, Annie. *Jean LeClerc (1657–1736) et la république des lettres.* Paris, 1938.

Bastide, Charles. "Bayle est-il l'auteur de *l'Avis aux réfugiés?*" *Bulletin de la Société de l'histoire du protestantisme français,* LVI (1907), 544–558.

"Bayle and his Dictionary," *The Literary Supplement (London Times),* April 24 (1953), p. 268.

Bayle, Pierre. Autograph Letters of Pierre Bayle. Columbia University MS.

——. Unpublished Letters of Pierre Bayle. Leyden University MS., Marchandi Codex No. 4.

——. *Addition aux "Pensées diverses sur les comètes," ou Réponse à un libelle intitulé "Courte Revue des maximes de morale et des principes de religion de l'auteur des "Pensées diverses sur les comètes." Pour servir d'instruction aux juges ecclésiastiques qui en voudraient connaître.* Rotterdam, 1694.

——. *Avis au petit auteur des petits livrets sur son "Philosophe dégradé."* [Rotterdam], 1691.

————. *La Cabale chimérique, ou réfutation de l'histoire fabuleuse qu'on vient de publier malicieusement touchant un certain projet de paix et touchant le libelle intitulé "Avis important aux réfugiés."* [Rotterdam], 1691.

————. *Ce que c'est que la France toute catholique sous le règne de Louis le Grand.* [Amsterdam], 1686.

————. *Chimère de la cabale de Rotterdam.* Rotterdam, 1691.

————. *Commentaire philosophique sur ces paroles de Jésus-Christ: "Contrains-les d'entrer;" où l'on prouve par plusieurs raisons démonstratives qu il n'y a rien de plus abominable que de faire des conversions par la contrainte, et l'apologie que saint Augustin a faite des persécutions.* Cantorbury [i.e., Amsterdam], 1686–1687.

————. *Critique générale de "l'Histoire du calvinisme" de M. Maimbourg.* Villefranche [i.e. Amsterdam], 1682.

————. *Déclaration de M. Bayle touchant la "Courte Revue des maximes."* Rotterdam, 1691.

————. *Dictionnaire historique et critique.* 1st ed. 2 vols. Rotterdam, 1697.

————. *Dictionnaire historique et critique.* 3rd ed. 4 vols. Rotterdam, 1720.

————. *Entretiens sur le grand scandale causé par un livre intitulé "La Cabale chimérique."* Cologne [i.e. Rotterdam], 1691.

————. *Janua coelorum reserata cunctis religionibus.* Rotterdam, 1692.

————. *Lettre à M.L.A.D.C., docteur de Sorbonne: Où il est prouvé par plusieurs raisons tirées de la philosophie et de la théologie que les comètes ne sont point le présage d'aucun malheur. Avec plusieurs réflexions morales et politiques et plusieurs observations historiques et la réfutation de quelques erreurs populaires.* Cologne [i.e. Rotterdam], 1682.

————. *Lettre sur les petits livrets publiés contre la "Cabale chimérique."* [Rotterdam], 1691.

————. *Lettres choisies de Bayle,* ed. Prosper Marchand. 3 vols. Rotterdam, 1714.

————. "Lettres de M. Bayle à sa famille," in *Oeuvres diverses,* Vol. I. Separately paginated. Rotterdam, 1737.

————. *Nouvel avis au petit auteur des petits livrets.* Rotterdam, 1692.

————. *Nouvelle hérésie dans la morale touchant la haine du prochain.* Rotterdam, 1964.

————. *Nouvelles de la République des Lettres.* Rotterdam, March 1684–February 1687.

————.*Nouvelles Lettres de l'auteur de la "Critique générale de l'Histoire du calvinisme de M. Maimbourg." Première partie, où en justifiant quelques endroits qui ont semblé contenir des contradictions, de faux raisonnements et autres méprises semblables, on traite par occasion de plusieurs choses curieuses qui ont du rapport à ces matières.* Villefranche [i.e. Amsterdam], 1685.

————. *Nouvelles Lettres de M. Pierre Bayle.* 2 vols. La Haye, 1739.

————. *Oeuvres diverses de M. Pierre Bayle, professeur en philosophie, et en histoire, à Rotterdam: Contenant tout ce que cet auteur a publié sur des matières de théologie, de philosophie, de critique, d'histoire, et de littérature; excepté son "Dictionnaire historique et critique."* 2nd ed. 4 vols. La Haye, 1737.

―――. *Pensées diverses sur la comète,* ed. A. Prat. Paris, 1911.

―――. *Projet et fragments d'un dictionnaire critique.* Rotterdam, 1692.

―――. *Suite des réflexions sur un imprimé qui a pour titre: "Jugement du public et particulièrement de M. l'Abbé Renaudot sur le Dictionnaire critique de M. Bayle."* Rotterdam, 1698.

―――. *Supplément du "Commentaire philosophique," où entre autres choses on achève de ruiner la seule échappatoire qui restait aux adversaires, en démontrant le droit égal des hérétiques pour persécuter à celui des orthodoxes. On parle aussi de la nature et de l'origine des erreurs. Hambourg* [i.e. Amsterdam], 1688.

Belin, J. P. *Le Commerce des livres prohibés à Paris de 1750 à 1789.* [No place], 1913.

Betz, Louis P. *Pierre Bayle und die "Nouvelles de la république des lettres."* Zurich, 1896.

Bolin, Wilhelm. *Pierre Bayle, sein Leben und seine Schriften.* Stuttgart, 1905.

Bouvier, Emile. "Contribution à l'étude des sources du *Siècle de Louis XIV,*" *Revue d'histoire littéraire de la France,* XLV (1938), 364–371.

Bredvold, Louis I. *The Intellectual Milieu of John Dryden: Studies in some Aspects of Seventeenth-century Thought.* Ann Arbor, Michigan, 1934.

Brown, Harcourt. "Pierre Bayle and Natural Science: An Unpublished Letter to Robert Boyle," *The Romanic Review,* XXV (1934), 361–367.

Browne, Thomas. *Religio medici,* ed. Jean-Jacques Denonian. Cambridge, England, 1955.

Brunetière, Ferdinand. "La Critique de Bayle," in *Etudes critiques sur l'histoire de la littérature française.* 5th series, 2nd ed., 5 vols. Paris, 1896.

Calvin, John. *Commentaries on the First Book of Moses called Genesis,* trans. John King. Grand Rapids, Michigan, 1948.

―――.*Institution de la religion Chrestienne,* ed. Jean-Daniel Bénoit. 2 bks. Paris, 1957.

Carnus, Juliette. "The Cosmological System of Pierre Bayle," *Philosophy of Science,* VIII (1941), 585–597.

Cazes, Albert. *Pierre Bayle, sa vie, ses idées, son influence, son oeuvre.* Paris, 1950.

Chenu, Jules. *Catalogue des républiques des Elzevier.* [No place], 1842.

Courtines, Leo Pierre. "Bayle and his English Correspondents: Four Unpublished Letters," *The Romanic Review,* XXVII (1936), 104–109.

―――. "Bayle, Hume, and Berkeley," *Revue de littérature comparée,* XXI (1947), 416–428.

―――. *Bayle's relations with England and the English.* New York, 1938.

Cowdrick, Ruth E. *The Early Reading of Pierre Bayle and Its Relation to his Intellectual Development up to the Beginning of the Publication of the "Nouvelles de la République des Lettres."* Scottdale, Pa., 1939.

Crocker, Lester G. *An Age in Crisis: Man and World in Eighteenth Century Thought.* Baltimore, 1959.

————. "The Problem of Truth and Falsehood in the Age of Enlightenment," *Journal of the History of Ideas,* XIV (1953), 575–603.

De Crousaz, Jean-Pierre. *Examen du pyrrhonisme ancien et moderne.* La Haye, 1733.

Delbos, Victor. *La Philosophie française.* Paris, 1919.

Delvolvé, Jean. *Essai sur Pierre Bayle, religion critique et philosophie positive.* Paris, 1906.

Denis, J. *Bayle et Jurieu.* Caen, 1886.

Denis, Fr. Paul. "Lettres inédites de Pierre Bayle," *Revue d'histoire littéraire de la France,* XIX (1912), 422–453.

Deregibus, Arturo. "Motivi religiosi ed aspetti metafisici dello scetticismo de Pietro Bayle," *Il Saggiatore,* IV (1954), 242–288.

————. "Lo Scetticismo di Pietro Bayle," *Il Saggiatore,* III (1953), 168–198.

————. "Sul concetto di storia nel pensiero di Bayle," *Il Saggiatore,* I (1951), 49–87.

Deschamps, Arsène. *La Genèse du scepticisme érudit chez Bayle.* Liège, 1878.

Des Maizeaux, Pierre. "The Life of Mr. Bayle," in the *Dictionary Historical and Critical of Mr. Peter Bayle.* 2nd English ed. London, 1737.

Dibon, Paul. "Redécouverte de Bayle," in *Pierre Bayle, le philosophe de Rotterdam,* ed. Paul Dibon. Amsterdam, 1959.

Douen, Orentin. "Un Opuscule (anonyme) de Bayle," *Bulletin de la Société de l'histoire du protestantisme français,* XXXVII (1877), 94–95.

Dubois, Lucien. *Bayle et la tolérance.* Paris, 1902.

Faguet, Emile. *Le Dixhuitième Siècle; études littéraires.* Paris, 1890.

Gerig, J. L., and G. L. van Roosbroek. "Unpublished Letters of Pierre Bayle," *The Romanic Review,* XXII (1931), 210–217; XXIII (1932), 20–23, 117–128, 206–224, 312–320; XXIV (1933), 17–20, 210–222, 312–314; XXV (1934), 15–24, 341–360.

Gigas, Emile. *Choix de la correspondance inédite de Pierre Bayle, 1670–1706.* Copenhaguen, 1890.

————. "La Première Ebauche d'un ouvrage célèbre," *Bulletin de la Commission de l'histoire des églises wallonnes,* 2nd series, II (1896), 65–74.

Giraud, Victor. "Les Etapes du XVIIIe siècle. I. Du *Dictionnaire* de Bayle à *l'Encyclopédie,*" *Revue des deux mondes,* XXII (1924), 344–375.

Gordon, Douglas H., and Norman L. Torrey. *The Censoring of Diderot's "Encyclopédie" and the Re-established Text.* New York, 1947.

Groethuysen, Bernard. "Bayle," *Mesures,* III (1937), 75–85.

Haase, Erich. *Einführung in die Literatur des Refuge: Der Beitrag der französischen Protestanten zur Entwicklung analytischer Denkformen am Ende des 17. Jahrhunderts.* Berlin, 1959.

Hanzeli, Victor E. "Pierre Bayle et la Hongrie," *French Review,* XXVII (1954), 346–353.

Hatin, Eugène. *Les Gazettes de Hollande et la presse clandestine aux XVIIe et XVIIIe siècles.* Paris, 1865.

————. *Manuel théorique et pratique de la liberté de la presse.* Paris, 1886.

Hawkins, R. L. "Two Unpublished French Letters: Pierre Bayle to Gilles Ménage," *The Romanic Review,* XXIII (1932), 14–19.

Haxo, Henry E. "Pierre Bayle and his biographers," *Modern Language Notes,* XXXVII (1922), 55–56.

Hazard, Paul. *La Crise de la conscience européenne (1680–1715).* Paris, 1961. Fayard edition.

————. *La Pensée européenne au XVIIIe siècle de Montesquieu à Lessing.* 3 vols. Paris [1946].

Hazewinkel, H. C. "Pierre Bayle à Rotterdam," in *Pierre Bayle, le philosophe de Rotterdam,* ed. Paul Dibon. Amsterdam, 1959.

Huetz de Lemps, R. "Pierre Bayle et le catholicisme," *La Pensée catholique,* XXIX (1954), 66–82.

Irwin, Beth L. "A Study of the Eschatological Preaching of Two Seventeenth-century French Calvinists." (Thesis, University of Wisconsin.) 1958.

James, E. D. "Scepticism and Fideism in Bayle's *Dictionnaire,*" *French Studies,* XVI (1962), 308–323.

Janmart de Brouillant, Léonce. *La Liberté de la presse en France aux XVIIe et XVIIIe siècles — Histoire de Pierre Marteau.* Paris, 1888.

Jeanmaire, Emile. *Essai sur la critique religieuse de Bayle.* Strasbourg, 1862.

Joly, Philippe-Louis. *Remarques critiques sur le "Dictionnaire" de Bayle.* 2 vols. Paris, 1752.

Jurieu, Pierre. *The Accomplishment of the Scripture Prophecies, or the Approaching Deliverance of the Church.* English trans. London, 1687.

————. *Nouvelle Hérésie dans la morale dénoncée au pape et aux évesques, aux princes et aux magistrats.* La Haye, 1689.

————. *La Religion des jésuites, ou réflexions sur les inscriptions du Père Menestrier et sur les escrits du Père le Tellier pour les nouveaux chrétiens de la Chine et des Indes contre la dixneuvième observation de "L'Esprit de M. Arnaud."* La Haye, 1689.

Kan, J. B. "Bayle et Jurieu," *Bulletin de la Commission de l'histoire des églises wallonnes,* 1st series, II (1889), 139–202.

————. "Lettres inédites de Pierre Bayle," *Bulletin de la Commission de l'histoire des églises wallonnes,* 2nd series, II (1898), 279–288.

Klibansky, Raymond, and H. J. Paton, eds. *Philosophy and History: Essays Presented to Ernst Cassirer.* 12 vols. Oxford, 1936.

Knuttel, Willem P. C. *Verboden Boeken in de Republiek der Vereenigde Nederlanden.* 's-Gravenhage, 1914.

Labrousse, Elisabeth. "Les Coulisses du journal de Bayle," in *Pierre Bayle, le philosophe de Rotterdam,* ed. Paul Dibon. Amsterdam, 1959.

————. "Documents relatifs à l'offre d'une chaire de philosophie à Bayle à l'Université de Franeker au printemps de 1684," in *Pierre Bayle, le philosophe de Rotterdam,* ed. Paul Dibon. Amsterdam, 1959.

————.*Inventaire critique de la correspondance de Pierre Bayle.* Paris, 1961.

————. *Pierre Bayle. Vol. I* ("Du comté de Foix à la cité d'Erasme"). La Haye, 1963.

————. *Pierre Bayle. Vol. II* ("Hétérodoxie et rigorisme") La Haye, 1964.

Lacoste, Edmond. *Bayle nouvelliste et critique littéraire, suivi d'une nouvelle édition des pamphlets de Bayle contre le maréchal de Luxembourg.* Paris, 1929.

Lanfrey, Pierre. *L'Eglise et les philosophes au XVIIIe siècle.* Paris, 1855.

Lanson, Gustave. "Bayle" in "Origines et premières manifestations de l'esprit philosophique dans la littérature française de 1675 à 1748," *Revue des cours et conférences,* XVI (1908), 629–637, 738–752, 817–829.

Lenient, Charles. *Etude sur Bayle.* Paris, 1855.

Lévy-Bruhl, Lucien. "Pierre Bayle," *Open Court,* XII (1898), 653–663.

MacPherson, Harriet D. *Censorship under Louis XIV (1661–1715).* New York, 1929.

Magnino, Bianca. "Genesi e significato dello scetticismo di Pietro Bayle," *Giornale critica della filosofia italiana,* XXII (1941), 209–225, 289–305.

Mason, H. T. "Pierre Bayle's Religious Views," *French Studies,* XVII (1963), 205–217.

Mirandolle, R. N. L. "A propos d'une lettre de Pierre Jurieu," *Bulletin de la Commission de l'histoire des églises wallonnes,* 2nd series, II (1898), 237–270.

Murris, Rocloz. *La Hollande et les Hollandais au XVIIe et au XVIIIe siècles vus par les Français.* Paris, 1925.

Nedergaard, Leif. "La Genèse du 'Dictionnaire historique et critique' de Pierre Bayle," *Orbis Litterarum,* XIII (1958), 210–227.

Peignot, Gabriel. *Dictionnaire critique, littéraire, et bibliographique des principaux livres condamnés au feu, supprimés ou censurés: precédé d'un discours sur ces sortes d'ouvrages.* Paris, 1806.

―――. *Essai historique sur la liberté d'écrire chez les anciens et au moyen âge; sur la liberté de la presse depuis le XVe siècle.* Paris, 1832.

Pellissier, L. G. "Lettres de divers écrivains français," *Bulletin du bibliophile et du bibliothécaire,* LXX (1906), 113–132; 222–232; 281–290, 357–373; 399–411.

Pierre Bayle, le philosophe de Rotterdam, ed. Paul Dibon. Amsterdam, 1959.

Pieters, Charles. *Annales de l'imprimerie des Elsevier, ou histoire de leur famille et de leurs éditions.* Gand, 1858.

Popkin, R. H. *The History of Scepticism from Erasmus to Descartes.* Assen, The Netherlands, 1960.

―――. "Pierre Bayle's Place in 17th-century Scepticism," in *Pierre Bayle, le philosophe de Rotterdam,* ed. Paul Dibon. Amsterdam, 1959.

―――. "The Sceptical Crisis and the Rise of Modern Philosophy," *Review of Metaphysics,* VII (1953), 132–151; 307–332, 499–510.

―――. "Scepticism in the Enlightenment," *Studies on Voltaire and The Eighteenth Century,* XXIV/XXVII (1963), 1321–1345.

―――. "An Unpublished Letter of Pierre Bayle to Pierre Jurieu," in *Pierre Bayle, le philosophe de Rotterdam.* Ed. Paul Dibon. Amsterdam, 1959.

Pottinger, David T. *The French Book Trade in the Ancien Régime.* Cambridge, Mass., 1958.

Puaux, Frank. *Les Précurseurs français de la tolérance au XVIIe siècle.* Paris, 1880.

Randolph, M. C. "Pierre Bayle's Case Against Satire and Satirists," *Notes and Queries,* CLXXXI (1941), 310–311.

Rateni, Benito. "L'Interpretazione critica del Bayle alla luce degli studi più recenti," *Rassegna de filosofia*, I (1952), 239–251.

Ray, Jean. "Du *Dictionnaire* de Bayle aux *Lettres persanes*," *Revue philosophique de la France et de l'étranger*, CXXXII (1945), 72.

Reesink, Hendrika J. *Index analytique des "Nouvelles de la république des lettres,"* in *L'Angleterre et la littérature anglaise dans les trois plus anciens périodiques français de Hollande de 1684 à 1709*. Zutphen, 1931.

Rex, Walter. *Essays on Pierre Bayle and Religious Controversy*. La Haye, 1965.

———. "Pierre Bayle, Louis Tronchin et la querelle des donatistes: Etude d'un document inédit, *Bulletin de la Sociéte de l'histoire du protestantisme français*, CV (1959), 97–121.

———. "Pierre Bayle: The Theology and Politics of the Article on David," *Bibliothèque d'Humanisme et de Renaissance*, XXIV and XXV (1962, 1963), 168–190 and 366–403.

Robinson, Howard. *Bayle the Sceptic*. New York, 1931.

———. *The Great Comet of 1680: A Study in the History of Rationalism*. Northfield, Minnesota, 1916.

Sabatié, Léon. *La Censure*. Paris, 1908.

Saigey, Edmond. "La Théologie de Bayle," *Nouvelle Revue de théologie*, V (1860), 1–22.

Saint-Beuve, Charles Augustin. "Du génie critique de Bayle," [essay written in 1843] in *Portraits littéraires*. 3 vols. Paris [1862].

Sarton, George. "Bayle and Boyle: The Sceptical Chemist and the Sceptical Historian," *Chymia, Annual Studies in the History of Chemistry*, III (1950), 155–192.

Sayous, André. *Histoire de la littérature française à l'étranger*. 2 vols. Paris, 1853.

Schoell, T. "Pierre Bayle à propos de deux livres récents (Delvolvé et Cazes), avec quelques notes bibliographiques," *Bulletin de la Société de l'histoire du protestantisme français*, LVIII (1908), 359–375.

Serrurier, Cornelia. *Pierre Bayle en Hollande: Etude historique et critique*. Lausanne, 1913.

Siccama, Jacques. "A tous les coeurs bien nés, que la patrie est chère," in *La Hollande et la liberté de penser au XVIIe et au XVIIIe siècles*. Paris, 1884.

Simon, Richard. *A Critical History of the Text of the New Testament, Wherein is Firmly Established the Truth of Those Acts on which the Foundation of the Christian Religion is Laid*. English trans. 2 vols. London, 1689.

———. *A Critical History of the Old Testament*. English trans. 3 vols. London, 1682.

Smith, Horatio E. "Bayle and his Biographers," *Modern Language Notes*, XXVII (1912), 158–159.

———. *The Literary Criticism of Pierre Bayle*. Albany, 1912.

Souquet, Paul. "Pierre Bayle, libre penseur et politique (1647–1706)," *Révolution française, revue d'histoire moderne et contemporaine*, XVIII (1890), 97–124; 210–231.

Stockum, Wilhelmus Petrus van, Jr. *La Librairie, l'imprimerie, et la presse en Hollande à travers quatre siècles.* La Haye, 1910.

Sugg, Elisabeth. *Pierre Bayle, ein Kritiker der Philosophie seiner Zeit.* Leipzig, 1930.

Thijssen-Schouten, C. Louise. "La diffusion européenne des idées de Bayle," in *Pierre Bayle, le philosophe de Rotterdam,* ed. Paul Dibon. Amsterdam, 1959.

Voltaire, Francois Marie Arouet de. *Oeuvres complètes de Voltaire,* ed. Louis Moland. 52 vols. Paris, 1877–1885.

INDEX

Academies
    Franecker, 54
    Geneva, 17, 26–27, 40
    Puylaurens, 20, 31
    Saumur, 26, 30, 83, 111
    Sedan, 33, 40, 83
    Toulouse, 17, 21, 26–27
Addition aux Pensées diverses, 90
analyse de la foi, 56, 78
Apocalypse of St. John, 85, 86, 91
Arminians, 31, 76–77, 100
Atheism, 28, 35–37, 42–45, 53, 56, 89
Avis aux réfugiés, 86–87, 89

Bayle, Pierre
    Anti-clericalism, 108–109
    Conversion to Catholicism, vii, 17, 21
    Dialectic, 26–30, 36, 38–39, 52, 105–106, 110
    Education, 20–21, 26–29, 31–32
    Critical opinion of,
        eighteenth century, viii, 8–9, 81, 108
        nineteenth century, viii, 9–10, 17–18, 35–36, 49–50, 75, 108
        twentieth century, viii, ix, 11–15, 36, 75, 100–101, 108
    Family, 19–20, 22–23, 33, 49, 57, 69, 84, 112
    Influence of, vii, 7
    Intellectual curiosity, vii, 18, 31–32, 81–82
    Milieu, viii, ix, 12, 18–20, 40, 42, 92, 99–104
    Personal religion, 21–24, 33, 76–78, 95–96, 104, 110–113
    Quarrel with Jurieu, 81–93, 109
    Reconversion to the Reform, vii, 17, 22–24
    Re-evaluation of, ix, 12–14
    Sincerity, 6, 7, 12, 15, 99–106, 108–109
Bekker, Balthasar, 89, 95, 102–103

Biblical heroes
    Immorality of, 61, 63–64, 72, 91–92
Bossuet, Jacques (Bishop), 19, 92
Browne, Sir Thomas, 12

Cabale chimérique, 87–88, 104
Calvin, John, 3, 51, 63–64, 85
Calvinism
    Ethical orientation, 30, 42, 51, 58, 70–71, 77, 95, 108, 109, 112
    Inner divisions, 93–94, 103
    Isolation, 18–19
    Moral decline of, 12, 31, 47, 52, 90, 111
    Rationalism in, 26, 38–39, 57, 69, 71, 109
Cartesianism, 26–27, 53, 57, 60, 64, 68–69, 76, 108, 110–111
Catholicism
    Moral condition of, 37, 40, 42–44, 50–51, 52
Censorship, 96, 99–104
Ce que c'est que la France toute catholique sous le règne de Louis le Grand, 69
Chouet, Robert, 26
Claude, Jean, 19–20, 54
Commentaire philosophique, 28, 46, 58, 62, 69–73, 75–77, 78, 84, 86–87, 106, 109, 111
Criterium veritatis
    Definition, 2–3, 19–20, 29–30, 39
    Way of authority, 19, 21, 73, 76
    Way of conscience, 24–25, 46–47, 53, 65, 75–76, 84, 112
    Way of examination, 19, 20, 21–22, 51, 57, 64
    Way of reason, 4–7, 38–39, 53, 59, 64, 70
    Way of the scripture, 4, 19–20, 39–40, 50–51, 59–65, 68, 73–75, 95, 111
Critique générale de "l'Histoire du Calvinisme," 49–54, 60, 83, 86